6

The Role of the Federal Government in Financing Higher Education

1789

Paper $2.00   Library edition in cloth $3.00

ALICE M. RIVLIN

The Role of
the Federal Government
in Financing
Higher Education

THE BROOKINGS INSTITUTION ● WASHINGTON, D. C.

THE BROOKINGS INSTITUTION is an independent organization devoted to nonpartisan research, education, and publication in economics, government, foreign policy, and the social sciences generally. Its principal purposes are to aid in the development of sound public policies and to promote public understanding of issues of national importance.

The Institution was founded December 8, 1927, to merge the activities of the Institute for Government Research, founded in 1916, the Institute of Economics, founded in 1922, and the Robert Brookings Graduate School of Economics and Government, founded in 1924.

The general administration of the Institution is the responsibility of a self-perpetuating Board of Trustees. In addition to this general responsibility the By-Laws provide that, "It is the function of the Trustees to make possible the conduct of scientific research and publication, under the most favorable conditions, and to safeguard the independence of the research staff in the pursuit of their studies and in the publication of the results of such studies. It is not a part of their function to determine, control, or influence the conduct of particular investigations or the conclusions reached." The immediate direction of the policies, program, and staff of the Institution is vested in the President, who is assisted by an advisory council, chosen from the professional staff of the Institution.

In publishing a study, the Institution presents it as a competent treatment of a subject worthy of public consideration. The interpretations and conclusions in such publications are those of the author or authors and do not necessarily reflect the views of other members of the Brookings staff or of the administrative officers of the Institution.

Foreword

THE ACTIVE INTEREST of the federal government in higher education has been aroused in recent years as never before, primarily because of the critical importance of higher education to national security, technological progress, and economic growth. These pressing problems, like others, require highly trained personnel. American leadership in the coming years, and perhaps even American survival, depend in large measure on the provision of top-quality education beyond the high school level for a substantial fraction of American young people.

While few question the national interest in higher education, wide differences of opinion exist over the appropriate role of the federal government in expressing this interest and in providing funds for higher education. Considerable debate in Congress and in the press has occurred over the desirability of federal aid to colleges and to college students and over the appropriate forms of such aid. This debate is certain to continue and to grow even more lively in the next few years.

The purpose of this monograph is to contribute to the consideration of these issues by providing a background of the federal government's role in financing higher education, by outlining the history of federal programs, and pointing out the principal issues which must be resolved.

The author, Alice M. Rivlin, is a member of the economics staff of the Brookings Institution. Brookings is grateful to Dr. Rivlin for her contribution and to the many persons who were helpful to her in carrying out the study.

She and the Institution are particularly indebted to the following individuals who read the study in draft and made helpful comments: Homer D. Babbidge, Russell I. Thackrey, Charles V. Kidd, Elmer D. West, and Selma J. Mushkin.

The following members of the Brookings staff also read the study in draft and contributed many useful ideas: George A. Graham, Director of Governmental Studies, Ralph J. Watkins, Director of Economic Studies, Richard Goode, Lewis H. Kimmel, and Harold Orlans. Many others assisted by providing information. Virginia Parker's editing improved the manuscript considerably. To all we are grateful.

As in all Brookings studies, the findings and conclusions are those of the author, and do not necessarily represent the views of associates at Brookings, or of those persons from whom the author received assistance.

ROBERT D. CALKINS
President

September 1961

Contents

Tables

1

The 'Crisis' in Higher Education

THE WORD "EDUCATION" does not appear in the Constitution. Traditionally, the support of education in the United States has been primarily the responsibility of states, localities, and private citizens, not of the federal government. Nevertheless, early in its history, the federal government took steps to assist in the foundation and support of colleges and universities. Beginning in 1787, grants of federal lands were made to new states specifically for support of institutions of higher education. After 1862, further land grants were made for the support of agricultural and mechanical colleges. Later, Congress voted to pay an annual subsidy to these colleges and to cooperate with them in financing agricultural research and extension activities. Still later, the federal government began to aid in the construction of campus buildings—first at public institutions and later at private institutions. And it began financing college and university research on a large scale and helping students to pay for their education through student work programs, veterans' benefits, loans, and fellowships.

One purpose of this study is to review the history of federal concern with higher education from the earliest days of the nation to the beginning of the 1960's. Thus, chapters 2 through 7 trace the history of land grants and aid to the land grant colleges, federally financed research on college and university campuses, the various programs through which the federal government has aided students, federally financed construction at higher educational institutions,

1

and the way in which the federal government has used both civilian institutions and its own academies for military education.

The second, and perhaps more important, purpose of the study is to raise and discuss fundamental questions about the future role of the federal government in financing higher education. Why should any level of government subsidize higher education? In particular, why and to what extent should the federal government do so? If there should be federal aid to higher education, should it go to students or to institutions? Should church-related institutions be aided? Should the aid be in the form of loans or grants? Should the loans or grants be earmarked for specific types of education of special national importance, or should such decisions be left to recipients of the aid? These questions are discussed in the last two chapters.

Although these are not new questions, it seems especially desirable just now to give serious thought to them. For one thing, federal programs involving higher education multiplied very rapidly in the 1950's, and it is time to take a look at the extent of this federal involvement and the reasons for it. More important, higher education will face a financial crisis in the 1960's, and the American people and their legislators are going to be called upon to decide, explicitly or by default, what role the federal government should play in resolving it.

We hear a great deal about this impending "crisis" in higher education. Why is there supposed to be a crisis? Although population is growing, national output is growing even faster. We, therefore, should be able to count on more and more resources for feeding, clothing, housing, educating, and otherwise providing for the needs of individuals.

There are two main reasons why the resources devoted to higher education will have to increase considerably faster in the next decade than national output is likely to increase, unless the American people are prepared to allow either a deterioration in the quality, or stricter limits on the availability, of higher education. One of the reasons relates to the age distribution of population growth and the other to the nature of the costs of higher education.

Growing Demand for Higher Education

The college-age group—persons 18 to 21 years old—is expected to grow in the United States from about 9.6 million in 1960 to about 14.6 million in 1970, or an average of about 4.3 per cent a year over a decade.[1] Thus, even if the cost per student remains constant, the resources going into higher education will have to increase more than 4 per cent each year. This rate of increase—slightly faster than gross national product has been increasing recently—would be needed to provide higher education for the same proportion of young people who are now obtaining it. By contrast, population in the main productive-age group (25 to 65 years of age) is expected to increase only from about 83.2 million to about 90.5 million between 1960 and 1970, or an average of less than 1 per cent per year.

There is little that is conjectural about the projections of college-age population to 1970. The children are already in elementary school and, barring nuclear disaster, only a very small and easily predictable fraction of them will fail to reach college age.

What is conjectural is the proportion of young people who will actually go to college. The ratio of total enrollment to college-age population rose rapidly from about 4 per cent in 1900 to around 15 per cent in 1940 to about 38 per cent (3.7 million students) in 1960. There is, of course, nothing immutable about this upward trend, and what happens in the future will depend on the policies adopted by governments, educational institutions, and families. The ratio may not rise further—and may even decline—if colleges and universities decide, instead of expanding facilities, to limit enrollment by raising tuition or entrance requirements or both. However, there is every reason to expect that, if colleges and universities as a group continue to make higher education available on approximately the present terms, the ratio of enrollment to college-age population will continue to increase. Perhaps, by 1970, it could be as much as 50 per cent (7.3 million students), perhaps more. This expectation is based mainly on the observation that at present a boy or girl who graduates from high school is most likely to go to college if his

[1] U. S. Bureau of the Census, *Current Population Reports*, Series P-25, No. 187, p. 4.

family's income is high, if he lives in a city rather than in a rural community, and if his parents went to college. Hence, as the average family income continues to rise, as urbanization continues, and as the increasing proportion of parents who had some higher education is reflected in the background of college-age youth, more young people may be expected to go to college. That is, they will go unless colleges ration admission by making it more expensive (relative to family income) or otherwise less available. Several recent studies indicate that a large proportion (well over 50 per cent) of parents with young children say they expect these children to go to college. However, it is impossible to evaluate the firmness of these expectations.[2]

Increasing Costs of Higher Education

Probable increases in the number of students form only part of the picture. The cost of higher education per student also seems likely to increase. Compared to other industries, higher education uses a great deal of labor, of highly skilled labor, to turn out its product. By far the largest item in the budget of an educational institution is salaries. If real wages and salaries continue to rise in the rest of the economy, colleges and universities will have to increase salary levels at least as rapidly. Otherwise, they will not be able to recruit and hold enough faculty members to teach larger numbers of students without a significant lowering of the average qualifications and training of teachers.

During the first half of this century, the incomes of college teachers failed to increase as rapidly as those of persons in most other occupations. In fact, the real income after taxes of the average full professor at a state university was actually less in 1953 than in 1904. College teachers made appreciable gains in real income in the late 1950's, but not enough to restore them to their relative position at the turn of the century.[3]

[2] See, for example, John B. Lansing *et al.*, *How People Pay for College*, University of Michigan, Survey Research Center, September 1960, p. 100.

[3] Sidney G. Tickton, *Teaching Salaries Then and Now—A Second Look*, Fund for the Advancement of Education, 1961.

The problem is not one simply of justice to the teaching profession. If well-trained people were so enamoured of the academic life and its nonpecuniary benefits that they continued to flock into college teaching, despite the deterioration in the relative income of college teachers, there would be little cause for concern. However, there is evidence that the average qualifications of faculty members (measured by the proportion who hold advanced degrees) have declined in recent years.[4] To reverse this trend and to provide instruction for more students, faculty salaries probably will have to rise faster in the future than real incomes generally. This means cost per college student is likely to rise considerably faster than other prices if present faculty-student ratios are maintained.

It is possible, of course, that in higher education—as in other industries—ways can be found of reorganizing the processes of production (or instruction) in order to economize on expensive factors (in this case, faculty time) and produce equally effective results at a lower cost per student. Some provocative suggestions have been made for economizing on faculty in a liberal arts college by reducing the number of courses offered and combining very large lectures with smaller discussion groups.[5]

It may prove possible to substitute for some faculty members capital equipment, such as closed circuit television installations or "teaching machines," at a long-run saving in cost and no detriment to the educational process. These possibilities should be systematically and energetically explored. But it now seems doubtful that ways can be found of economizing faculty time sufficiently to offset the necessary rise in salaries and to keep cost per student constant without lowering the quality of education. Moreover, the rapidity with which human knowledge is growing necessitates a constant improvement in the quality of education—more must be learned in the same amount of time, if formal education is not to be prolonged into middle age. This improvement probably cannot be achieved without increasing the resources per student devoted to higher education. Laboratories and other physical facilities must be mod-

[4] National Education Association, *Teacher Supply and Demand in Universities, Colleges, and Junior Colleges, 1959-60 and 1960-61,* May 1961, Table 4.

[5] Beardsley Ruml and Donald H. Morrison, *Memo to a College Trustee,* McGraw-Hill, 1959.

ernized, libraries must be expanded, faculty members must receive more training at the start of their careers (not less, as is the current trend) and they must take more time from teaching to keep up with the rapid changes in their disciplines.

If the number of students doubles in the next decade—which is not unlikely—and the cost of educating a student increases by 25 per cent—which seems conservative—current resources devoted to higher education 10 years from now will have to be two and a half times as great as at present. This means they will have to increase by more than 10 per cent per year, which is at least twice as fast as the rate at which optimists think our total production is likely to grow in the same period. Clearly, some serious thought needs to be given to what role, if any, the federal government ought to play in facilitating this rapid transfer of resources.

The Plight of Private
Colleges and Universities

A sub-crisis in higher education is created by the special problems of private colleges and universities, especially small liberal arts colleges. As the costs of providing higher education have risen, private institutions as a group have found themselves in an increasingly precarious financial position. Low interest rates—compared to 40 or 50 years ago—have kept endowment earnings down, and high income and estate taxes have cut into the private fortunes which once went as bequests to private colleges and universities. As public institutions of higher education have become widely available, many church groups have lost interest in supporting colleges they originally founded and helped to finance. Thus, private colleges have been forced to raise student fees in an effort to cover rising costs, but those that are less well-known have found they could not raise fees appreciably without losing students (often their best ones) to the heavily subsidized state institutions. As a result, many private institutions, especially the small ones, have not been able to raise faculty salaries to levels which would allow them to compete with public institutions for well-qualified faculty members. In many, buildings have fallen into disrepair and laboratories and equipment have become outmoded.

Private institutions enrolled about 41 per cent of all college and university students in 1959. There has been a decline in this proportion since 1939—in that year, about 54 per cent were enrolled in private institutions—a decline partly attributable to the rapid growth of public junior colleges. Although there are almost twice as many private institutions as public ones, many are small. In 1955, out of 1,858 institutions of higher education in the United States, 1,203 were privately controlled, and 958 of these enrolled less than a thousand students.

Many persons view the financial distress of private colleges as a disaster for American higher education in general. A large number of private institutions, including some small ones, have been leaders in raising standards, experimenting with new methods, and providing enclaves for free thought in periods when zeal for conformity was sending state legislative investigating committees on the rampage. The diversity of American higher education, providing opportunities for different types of students to find institutions suited to their particular needs, has been one of its strengths. Private colleges and universities have contributed a great deal to this diversity and vitality.

Moreover, the case for these private institutions does not rest only on past glories. Its advocates are quick to point out the stupidity of letting private colleges deteriorate at a time when rising enrollment indicates the need for rapid expansion of higher educational facilities. In many instances, they argue, it would be sensible to utilize, expand, and improve facilities that already exist before setting up new ones. Since most states are too heavily committed to public institutions to be willing to assist private ones, many persons have suggested that the federal government ought to expand its support of higher education in ways that would be of particular benefit to private institutions.

This view is by no means unanimous. Many point out that the private colleges most in need of help are too small to be efficient, that their standards are often low and their curricula limited, and that subsidizing these small institutions—like subsidizing the family farm—is a sentimental, but uneconomic, use of national resources. Further, they believe public funds should be subject to firm public control and that aiding private church-related institutions jeopardizes the principle of separation of church and state.

These issues are significant in themselves. However, the most important reason for reconsidering the role of the federal government in financing higher education is the now widespread, yet comparatively recent, realization of how important higher education is to national economic and military strength. Both our military capacity and the economic growth on which it partially depends have become vitally linked to rapid advances in research, and to the availability of highly trained manpower to carry out the research and to utilize the results. This clearly makes higher education a major national concern. It does not necessarily point to the conclusion that substantial increases in federal funds provide the optimum solution. But it certainly points up the need for some hard thinking about what role the national government should play in financing higher education.

GENERAL REFERENCES

1) John S. Brubacher and Willis Rudy, *Higher Education in Transition; An American History: 1636-1956,* Harper, 1958.
2) Hollis P. Allen, *The Federal Government and Education,* McGraw-Hill, 1950.
3) Richard G. Axt, *The Federal Government and Financing Higher Education* (published for the Commission on Financing Higher Education), Columbia University Press, 1952.
4) The American Assembly, *The Federal Government and Higher Education,* Prentice-Hall (Spectrum Books), 1960.
5) Dexter M. Keezer (ed.), *Financing Higher Education, 1960-70,* McGraw-Hill, 1959.

2

State Universities and Land Grant Colleges

THE HISTORY of federal participation in financing higher education in the United States goes back to the beginnings of the Republic. In the first hundred years, however, participation was relatively simple. With minor exceptions, such as the establishment of military academies, federal support of higher education before 1890 was confined to a single form—the granting of public lands to the states to support "seminaries," colleges, and universities. Since the closing years of the nineteenth century, the range of federal activities has expanded to include direct loans and grants to institutions, fellowships and loans for students, research contracts, extension programs, and a wide variety of other forms of federal involvement in higher educational finance.

The First Federal Land Grants

The first federal land grants for higher education were in the Northwest Territory. At the close of the Revolutionary War the new Congress had large war debts and meager sources of revenue. The region between the Appalachians and the Mississippi River north of the Ohio was part of the newly independent Confederation, but was claimed by several of the states. In order to dispose of the conflicting claims and, at the same time, to give the central government an important source of funds with which to pay off its

9

obligations, the Congress invited the states involved to cede their claims to the national government. A resolution was adopted in 1780 declaring that the ceded territory would be used for the national benefit and would eventually be formed into new states. Within the next six years, New York, Virginia, Massachusetts, and Connecticut relinquished their claims to the disputed territory, and Congress proceeded to consider various proposals for turning its new asset into cash.

The suggestion that some of the land should be devoted to the support of education is known to have been made as early as 1783. In that year, a group of New England army officers sent a petition to Congress calling for the establishment of a new state in the Northwest Territory. The group suggested that part of the land in the new state be distributed to war veterans and part be turned over to the new state to cover the costs of government, "schools and academies," and other public works. Neither this petition nor a somewhat similar proposal made by a Colonel Bland of Virginia was acted upon by the Congress. In 1785, however, an ordinance was passed which provided for the surveying of the territory, and for its division into townships six miles square, within each of which one square mile was to be reserved for the maintenance of public schools.

In setting aside land to be used for public schools, Congress does not seem to have been motivated primarily by a desire to use federal resources to aid education. There certainly was no important group in the Congress which wished to make education a concern of the central government. The main hope was to sell the new public lands quickly and at as advantageous a price as possible, in order to bring money into the empty treasury. The provision for schools was viewed as a means of inducing settlers, especially those from education-conscious New England, to leave their homes and buy land in the wilderness. In fact, before it could dispose of the land, Congress was forced to make even greater concessions to education in the new Territory.

A group of New Englanders, including some of the persons associated with the army officers' petition of 1783, conceived the idea of buying a substantial piece of land in the Northwest Territory and offering it to Revolutionary War veterans. They formed the Ohio Company, sold stock on the open market and, in 1787, sent a delegation to Congress to negotiate for the sale of land. Dr. Manasseh Cutler, principal spokesman for the company, seems to have felt strongly that provision for schools and churches would enhance the attractiveness of the Territory to New England settlers, and he drove a hard bargain with the congressional committee over the terms of the sale. Not satisfied with the reservation of a square mile in each township for public schools, he demanded a similar section in each township for religion and four whole townships for a university.

At first, Congress was unwilling to go this far, but the prospect of disposing of a very large quantity of land (2 million acres) in a single transaction was very attractive, and it finally agreed to most of Cutler's demands. An ordinance of July 23, 1787, authorized sale of the land to the Ohio Company and set aside one square mile in each township for public schools, one for religion, and two townships of good land near the center of the purchase "for the support of a literary institution, to be applied to the intended object by the legislature of the State." This first federal grant for higher education eventually provided an endowment for Ohio University at Athens, Ohio.

Later in the same year, the Treasury made a contract with one John Cleve Symmes for the sale of a somewhat smaller tract of land in what is now southwestern Ohio. Again, as a condition of the sale, the national government agreed to set aside land for public schools and to grant a whole township to the state for higher education. This grant was to result, after many vicissitudes, in the establishment of Miami University.

By this time, it may have been clear to Congress that granting university townships to the territories as part of contracts for the sale of lands to private persons was not likely to result in the best national distribution of educational facilities. In any case, the policy was not continued. The grants already made in Ohio were confirmed in the act enabling Ohio to become a state in 1802. Two years later, Congress established three land districts within the remaining portion of the Northwest Territory and set aside one township in each district for a "seminary." These three seminary townships were eventually granted to the three new states of Indiana, Illinois, and Michigan, together with one additional township in each state. A precedent was thus established, and thereafter each new state which entered the Union (except Maine and Texas which had no federal lands) received a land grant for a seminary or university.[1] Most of the states received two townships (46,080 acres) or their equivalent, but Wisconsin, Minnesota, and Florida managed to obtain twice this amount, and some of the western states which came late into the Union received larger acreages. Arizona and New Mexico, for example, received 200,000 acres each for the support of a university.

The management of these land grants by the states was often wasteful, even fraudulent, especially in the early years. Frequently the state legislatures were more eager to further the interests of prospective purchasers or tenants than to safeguard the university endowments. In Ohio, a seemingly excellent system was originally provided. The trustees of Ohio University were to have the land valued by an impartial commission and then lease it on a long-term basis, subject to revaluation after 35 years, using the revenue for the support of the University. After passing this law, however, the legislature became concerned about the interests of the University's tenants and passed another act which made no mention of revaluation. When the 35 years had elapsed and the value of the lands had appreciated greatly, the University attempted to have them revalued, but met with strenuous objections from the tenants. The case reached the Supreme Court of Ohio which decided for the University, but the legislature immediately countered with a law forbidding the revaluations. As a result, the very valuable lands held by Ohio and Miami Universities produced almost negligible revenues for the two institutions.

In most of the states, the university lands were sold rather than leased, and all too often the legislatures rushed into hasty sales and realized far less than the true market value of the lands. In Michigan, the legislature favored the squatters already on the lands and required the University to sell to them at less than the market price.

[1] Texas had substantial state lands, part of which were used for university endowment.

In Indiana, the small proceeds of too hasty sales were unwisely invested and further losses ensued. In view of this early history, it is perhaps surprising that Congress waited until 1875 (in the enabling act for Colorado) before specifying a minimum price below which these lands should not be sold.

The state enabling acts specified only that the land was to be used for "seminaries of learning" or "a university." The nature of the institutions to be supported was left entirely to the legislatures of the states. The early statutes did not even say that the institution should be publicly controlled. In most cases, the legislatures did retain control of the institutions they created—at least through reserving the power to appoint the trustees. Indiana, however, transferred one of its seminary townships to Vincennes University, a church-related institution with a self-perpetuating board of trustees. In later years, Congress specified that the institutions endowed with the federal grants should be state-controlled.

The case of Illinois is significant because it illustrates the almost complete absence of federal control over the use of these grants. Illinois, which received two seminary townships when it was admitted to the Union in 1818, sold most of the land relatively soon. However, no university was founded for almost 40 years. From 1835 until the Illinois Normal University was founded in 1857, the interest on the university fund was used for the public schools—in flagrant violation of the provisions of the federal grant.

Despite the comparatively small sums realized from the federal land grants and the instances of early mismanagement, the importance of these grants to the development of state universities in the Middle West and Far West should not be underestimated. In state after state, institutions of higher learning were founded in order to take advantage of the federal grants. Often these "universities" were scarcely more than high schools, but they were the foundations on which the states were later to build strong state universities. It seems likely that without the stimulation of the federal grants many states would have had no public institution of higher education—and some no higher educational institutions at all—until many years later.

The Morrill Act and the Land Grant Colleges[2]

A new chapter in the history of federal aid to higher education began with the passage of the Morrill Act in 1862. Although the measure continued the long-standing policy of granting federal lands to the states for the support of higher education, it was a departure in several respects. For one thing all states, even those with no public lands, shared in the federal bounty, and the distribution was made roughly on the basis of population. Each state received 30,000 acres (or the equivalent in land scrip) for each senator or congressman to which it was entitled. Second, the type of education to be aided was specified in the act. The interest on the funds realized from the sale of the land (or scrip) was to be devoted to

> the endowment, support, and maintenance of at least one college where the leading object shall be without excluding other scientific and classical studies, and including military tactics, to teach such branches of learning as are related to agriculture and the mechanic arts. . . .

This does not sound very specific by modern standards, but it was a marked contrast to earlier federal legislation, which had made no reference to what was to be taught in the institutions established. The stated objective of the Morrill Act was not to aid higher education in general, but to "promote the liberal and practical education of the industrial classes in the several pursuits and professions in life."

Furthermore, the Morrill Act imposed certain definite obligations on a state which accepted the grant. It had to have an agricultural and mechanical college in existence within five years; it had to dispose of the land or scrip and safeguard the proceeds as a perpetual endowment from which the college was to receive an income of not less than 5 per cent; and it had to make an annual report to Washington. Moreover, since none of the Morrill Act money could be used for buildings, the states which did not already have colleges

---

[2] The term "land grant college" has come to mean those institutions benefitting from the provisions of the Morrill Act.

(and most of them did not) were effectively accepting an obligation to put their own money into physical plants. This might be considered the genesis of the idea of joint financing of educational ventures, which was to culminate in the "matching" provisions of later federal legislation in support of higher education.

The author of the measure, Justin S. Morrill, Representative (and later Senator) from Vermont, seems to have had a strong desire to "do something for agriculture" by providing educational opportunities for future farmers. He did not make clear exactly what kind of education he thought the farmers should have—perhaps he was not sure himself—except that it was to be more practical and more meaningful to the tillers of the soil and the rest of the "industrial classes" than the classical studies offered in the traditional colleges.

In this desire, Morrill certainly was not alone. The first half of the nineteenth century had witnessed growing dissatisfaction with the existing colleges, whose narrow curricula were primarily designed to give future professional men a thorough grounding in classical studies. Even pure science was sadly neglected, and courses in the practical application of scientific knowledge to agricultural and industrial problems were virtually nonexistent. To meet this need, a number of private technical schools already had been founded—most of them outside the established colleges. Of these, Rensselaer Polytechnic Institute was the most notable. At the same time, the growing movement for a more scientific agriculture had resulted in the foundation of a number of agricultural schools and colleges.

Most of the private agricultural schools were inadequately financed and folded up not long after they started, but by 1862 several state-supported agricultural schools were also operating or in the process of being established. By far the most important was the Michigan Agricultural College in East Lansing (now Michigan State University), which was founded in 1855 and served as a model for many of the land grant colleges. In the same year, the legislature of Pennsylvania founded the Farmers' High School, forerunner of Pennsylvania State College (now Pennsylvania State University). Maryland also had a functioning state school of agriculture before the passage of the Morrill Act, and the legislatures of Iowa and Massachusetts had provided for the creation of institutions.

Despite growing recognition of the need for higher education in agriculture and industry and increasing support for federal aid in the field, the Morrill Act was not passed without long and acrimonious debate.

Efforts to Pass the Morrill Act

As early as 1856, in his first term in Congress, Morrill introduced a resolution asking the Committee on Agriculture to consider the establishment of "one or more national agricultural schools upon the basis of the U. S. Naval and Military schools, in order that one scholar from each congressional district and two from each state at large, may receive a scientific and practical education at public expense." The resolution apparently had little support and never reached a vote.

By the next session of Congress, however, Morrill had turned from the advocacy of an agricultural West Point to a plan for federal land grants to the states for agricultural and mechanical colleges, and he introduced a bill very similar to the one which eventually passed in 1862. In 1859, after repeated delays, impassioned debate— almost none of which concerned the merits of agricultural education—and some skillful parliamentary moves on the part of its sponsor, the first Morrill Bill passed both houses by small margins. However, it was vetoed by President Buchanan, and Morrill was unable to muster enough votes to override the veto.

Support for the measure came from several sources. First, there were those genuinely interested in agricultural education. The existing agricultural colleges were eager for federal assistance and were among the most active lobbyists for the legislation. Some farm organizations favored the Bill, although there is no evidence that the average farmer knew or cared about the plans. Concern for agricultural education, however, would never have carried the measure through Congress, without its provisions concerning public lands. Representatives of the older states of the Northeast, which had no public lands, were eager to establish the point that they, as well as the newer states, had a right to a share in the public domain. The Morrill Bill not only promised them a share of the public lands, but proposed distribution of the land on the basis of population—a distribution formula which favored the older states.

Opposition to the Bill came from western congressmen who were reluctant to let the eastern states participate in the distribution of lands within their borders and fearful that the land would be bought up by speculators in large blocks and withheld from actual settlers. They were joined by the "states' rights" congressmen from the South, who argued—as their descendants are still arguing—that federal aid to education in any form was both unconstitutional and undesirable. Buchanan's veto message stressed his view that the Bill was unconstitutional.

Undaunted by this reversal, Morrill reintroduced his Bill in late 1861. By this time the southern states were no longer represented in Congress, and, although many western congressmen were still strongly opposed, the Bill passed both houses by substantial margins in 1862, and was signed by President Lincoln. The Act originally excluded the southern states, but its benefits were extended to them after the Civil War, and later to new states and territories. The inclusion of "military tactics" in the subjects to be taught by the new colleges was a reflection of the concern felt over Union reversals in the early part of the War.

Establishment of Colleges Under the Act

Although the Morrill Act specified that the colleges to be aided should teach agriculture, military tactics, and the mechanic arts, little additional guidance was given to the states. The word "college" was used loosely in those days. It was not clear whether Congress had intended to create trade schools at essentially a high school level or genuine institutions of higher education in science and technology. Furthermore, the Act did not specify that the institutions should be publicly controlled, nor that the funds should be concentrated in a single institution within each state. This congressional vagueness resulted in varying arrangements by the states.

Michigan and the other states which had already taken steps to establish agricultural colleges designated those colleges as the recipients of the funds. Massachusetts divided its grant between a state agricultural college, forerunner of the University of Massachusetts, and a private institution, the Massachusetts Institute of Technology. Several other states, primarily in the Northeast where there was little sentiment for public education, originally designated private institutions as their land grant recipients. Among these were Brown in Rhode Island and the Sheffield School at Yale in Connecticut. In most of these cases, the funds were subsequently transferred to state-controlled institutions, although in a few instances—notably, Cornell in New York—a state-supported agricultural college was maintained within a private institution.

Some states, such as Wisconsin, designated the state university as the land grant college—a procedure which considerably strengthened their universities. In 1868, Minnesota, whose university was then weak and deeply in debt, passed an "Act to Reorganize the University of Minnesota and to Establish an Agricultural College Therein," to which the present University essentially owes its existence. Other states were stimulated by the Morrill Act to start universities. Illinois, which had no real state university, responded to the Morrill Act by establishing the Illinois Industrial University (later called the University of Illinois) in 1867.

Many of the states created state-controlled agricultural and mechanical colleges which probably would never have been established without the Act. Legislatures which had given no thought to agricultural and mechanical education were suddenly eager to establish some sort of college which would entitle them to share in the federal bounty—even if it meant the expenditure of state funds. They were often under considerable political pressure not to combine the agricultural college with the state university—pressure from agriculturalists who wanted the prestige of a separate institution or who feared the domination of classical scholars, and pressure from constituents who wanted new institutions located in their communities.

In many instances, the decision to separate the land grant college from the state university undoubtedly delayed the building of strong institutions of public higher education. In Iowa, where a state university was barely getting started at Iowa City, the legislature decided to found a separate agricultural and mechanical college in a different part of the state. In Kansas, the agricultural and mechanical college at Manhattan was founded before the state university. A year or so later, the legislature voted to found a state university in the same town, then yielded to political pressure and located it at Lawrence instead. For many years, neither of these states was in a position to support one institution of higher education adequately, let alone two. Similarly, Ohio, although it already had two small institutions barely managing to stay alive on the income from earlier federal land grants, used its federal grant to set up a third. The Ohio legislature asked local communities to enter bids for the agricultural and mechanical college. Franklin County, in which Columbus is situated, made the highest bid, with substantial contributions made by two of the railroads which passed through Columbus. Columbus turned out to be a very good location for Ohio State University, but the creation of a third state institution undoubtedly weakened the existing two.

In some states, private donors like Ezra Cornell and John Purdue supplemented the federal grant with substantial gifts. In many others the "A. and M." college struggled along for years on the income from the federal grant with negligible state support, few students, and no clear idea of its function. Only gradually did the states take over the responsibility for their support and build them into strong institutions of genuinely higher education—sometimes into the principal university of the state.

Further Support for Land Grant Colleges

If Congress had abandoned the support of the agricultural and mechanical colleges after passing the Morrill Act, they would have no more significance in this narrative than the many other institutions which received endowments of federal lands. Through a series of subsequent enactments, however, the federal government maintained close ties with the land grant colleges. The ties were of two kinds: annual subsidies for the general support of the land grant colleges, and utilization of these colleges to carry out federal programs of agricultural research and extension.

Annual Federal Subsidies

In 1890, Congress passed the second Morrill Act which provided for annual payments to the states for the support of the land grant colleges. The money was to be used for instruction in "agriculture, the mechanic arts, the English language, and the various branches of mathematical, physical, natural, and economic science, with special reference to their application in the industries of life."

These federal subsidies were of considerable help to the land grant colleges at the time they were instituted, but their recent significance lies more in their continued existence than in size. Although the annual appropriations were augmented in 1907 and again in 1935, by 1961 they totaled only about $5 million a year, which represented less than half of 1 per cent of the current aggregate income of the land grant colleges. Each of the 50 states received $70,000 a year, and an additional $1,501,500 was divided among them on the basis of population. (Puerto Rico got a flat $50,000.) Sums of this magnitude are scarcely detectable in the budgets of such major universities as Cornell, Purdue, and the University of California; they have more significance for some of the smaller institutions, such as the Universities of Nevada and Alaska and the Negro land grant colleges in the South.[3]

In July 1960, the 86th Congress passed Public Law 658 authorizing a substantial increase in the land grant college subsidies to begin in fiscal year 1962. If the appropriation is enacted as authorized, each state and Puerto Rico will receive a total of $200,000 a year, with an additional $4.3 million being divided on the basis of population, making a total of $14.5 million. At the time this was written, only $10.7 million had been appropriated for fiscal year 1962, although a supplementary appropriation might still be added.

[3] Seventeen southern states founded separate land grant colleges for Negroes. (One of these, West Virginia State College, has recently ceased to be a land grant college.) Three were established before 1890, but the rest were founded in order to comply with the provisions of the second Morrill Act which stated that federal funds would not be paid to states which discriminated against colored students in admissions to land grant colleges, but that the maintenance of separate institutions for Negroes would be considered adequate as long as the federal funds were "equitably" divided. This is one of the few instances in which the doctrine of separate but equal (or rather "separate but equitable") facilities was explicitly recognized in federal legislation.

Research and Extension Services

In 1887, Congress passed the Hatch Act establishing an agricultural experiment station in each state to undertake and report publicly on scientific experiments of importance to agriculture. The stations were located in the land grant colleges, and much of the research has been directed or carried out by faculty members. The experiment stations have received regular federal appropriations, but the states have also contributed to their support and over the years have gradually taken over a larger share of their budgets.[4]

The other important federal program involving the land grant colleges has been agricultural extension. Most of the colleges established some sort of extension work early in their history in order to carry the results of their work to the farmers and to learn more about local agricultural problems; and many had flourishing programs by 1914. Professors conducted institutes, short courses, and various kinds of demonstrations for farmers and their wives. During the same period, the U. S. Department of Agriculture was beginning to engage in extension and demonstration work of its own through county agents in rural areas, and some similar work was being done by state departments of agriculture.

In 1914, the Smith-Lever Act providing a means of merging these competing programs into a single cooperative venture was passed. The U. S. Department of Agriculture abandoned its independent extension program and offered to work through the land grant colleges. Congress appropriated money for the programs, but stipulated that the states which accepted the federal funds should put up an equal amount of money. This was the first federal law to contain a formal "matching" provision.

The cooperative agricultural extension service is now a widespread joint enterprise of the U. S. Department of Agriculture and the land grant colleges with over 10,000 county agents, assistants, and home demonstrators in over 3,000 counties. Their job is to distribute up-to-date information on farming methods, home economics, and agricultural marketing and to keep the colleges and the Department in touch with the farmers. States are still required

---

[4] The experiment stations are discussed in greater detail in chapter 3.

to match federal funds and, in fact, regularly appropriate more than the amounts required for matching.

There has been some pressure in recent years for extending federal support to land grant colleges for nonagricultural extension activities, such as evening classes for city dwellers and similar forms of adult education. Hearings were held in the House of Representatives on several bills to this effect in 1959 and 1960, but no action was taken.

The degree of control exercised by the federal government over the land grant colleges has varied in different phases of their activities. Both the experiment stations and the agricultural extension programs are under the jurisdiction of the U. S. Secretary of Agriculture, and the colleges are required to secure prior approval of their plans for expending federal funds for these purposes. However, in actual practice, the Department of Agriculture has allowed the stations great freedom both in making and carrying out their own research plans, intervening mainly to help coordinate activities among the states. With respect to the general teaching programs of the land grant colleges, the federal government has exercised almost no control at all. The college presidents are required to submit an annual report to the U. S. Office of Education showing how federal subsidies were spent in the previous year. The language of the second Morrill Act is so broad, and the sums involved are so small relative to the total income of the institutions, that none has any difficulty listing expenditures which are clearly within the scope of the legislation. There do not seem to have been any instances in which the federal government has dictated subject matter, or how or by whom courses should be taught.

SELECTED REFERENCES FOR CHAPTER 2

1) Howard C. Taylor, *The Educational Significance of the Early Federal Land Ordinances*, Teachers College, Columbia University, 1922.

2) Donald G. Tewksbury, *The Founding of American Colleges and Universities Before the Civil War*, Teachers College, Columbia University, 1932.
3) Earle D. Ross, *Democracy's College: The Land-Grant Movement in the Formative Stage*, Iowa State College Press, 1942.
4) Edward D. Eddy, Jr., *Colleges for Our Land and Time: The Land-Grant Idea in American Education*, Harper, 1956.
5) Richard G. Axt, *The Federal Government and Financing Higher Education*, Columbia University Press, 1952, chapters II and III.
6) U. S. Department of Health, Education and Welfare, Office of Education, *Statistics of Land Grant Colleges and Universities* (annual).

3

Federal Support of Research in Universities

RESEARCH AND DEVELOPMENT are by far the most important federally supported activities involving colleges and universities. At present, the federal government is spending over three-quarters of a billion dollars a year on research and development conducted by higher educational institutions—a sum which represents about two-thirds of the total expenditures of these institutions for research and development. While this may not be "aid to higher education" in the traditional sense, it has important fiscal and educational effects, especially on the larger institutions.

Up to 1940 federal support of university research was largely confined to support of agricultural research in the land grant colleges. During World War II the government began financing health and defense research in a wider group of colleges and universities and has continued to do so on an increasing scale in the Cold War period. New patterns of research support evolved—and are continuing to evolve—in the health and defense fields which contrast sharply with the patterns of support that grew up during the 70 years of federal experience with agricultural research support.

Agricultural Research

When the land grant colleges first began organizing courses in farming in the 1860's and 1870's they discovered there was very little to teach. Scientific agriculture was still in its infancy. In an

24

effort to build up useful courses, most of the colleges began informal research and experimentation soon after their foundation, and some organized formal "experiment stations" to conduct research and disseminate the results among the farmers in their states. By the 1880's the land grant colleges began to lobby for federal support of these activities, and their efforts eventually secured passage of the Hatch Act in 1887.

Under the Hatch Act, each state received an annual grant of $15,000 toward the support of an agricultural experiment station at its land grant college. The program was placed under the supervision of the U. S. Commissioner of Agriculture, and experiment stations were required to make an annual report to him. In general, they were expected to choose their own research projects, although the Commissioner was empowered "to indicate, from time to time, such lines of inquiry as to him shall seem most important."

The Adams Act of 1906 increased the federal contribution to the experiment stations and gave the U. S. Secretary of Agriculture more control over their expenditures. After this, the stations were required to secure prior approval of specific research projects for which they desired to use federal funds. Later legislation—in 1925, 1935, 1946, and 1955—further increased grants to the experiment stations and broadened the scope of their activities to include some problems of social science and some aspects of marketing research. The system of financing specific projects in the experiment stations, rather than giving general support to a research organization, was to become a characteristic feature of federal participation in university research in all fields.

State, as well as federal, support for the experiment stations has increased over the years. In fiscal year 1960, the states received about $31 million from the federal government for the experiment stations—divided partly on an equal basis and partly in proportion to the farm and rural populations of the states. Most of the states' contributions far exceeded requirements for matching federal funds, as illustrated by the fact that nonfederal funds for the support of the experiment stations in 1960 totaled about $112 million, or about 3.6 times the federal contribution. Of this, about $83 million was appropriated by the states and $29 million came from endowments, sales of agricultural products, and a variety of other sources.[1] The ratio of nonfederal to federal funds, however, differed widely by states. For example, in California and Florida, nonfederal funds were more than 10 times the federal grants while, in Vermont and New Hampshire, they were not much more than sufficient to match the federal funds.

The initiative for planning and carrying out research rests with the experiment stations; the Department of Agriculture regards itself primarily as a coordinator of the stations' work. The stations submit to the Department descriptions of the projects for which they intend to use their federal funds. These are reviewed by Department specialists, who check to see whether similar work has been done, or is in progress, at other stations or in the Department itself. While the Department has the right to reject station projects which it regards as unsound or unsuitable, this power is rarely exercised. The reviews, however, often result in revisions of proposed projects, especially revisions designed to avoid duplication of effort.

Although the Department of Agriculture occasionally makes research suggestions to the stations, as it has other research funds of its own, there is no need to press particular projects on the stations. On the other hand, the stations have little reason to ask for federal money for projects with which the Department is unsympathetic, since they have other sources of funds. In fact, this joint state-federal support has given the stations considerable independence from dictation by either level of government. Occasionaly, they have fallen back on federal support in their efforts to fend off what was considered undue political influence at the state level.[2]

Most of the federal money for research at agricultural experiment stations is distributed among the states on the basis of formulas specified by Congress. Since each state knows how much it is entitled to receive, the stations submit project proposals which will use up this money. The stations do not compete with each other for federal funds. Presumably the quality of work is higher at some

[1] U. S. Department of Agriculture, Agricultural Research Service, *Funds for Research at the State Agricultural Experiment Stations, 1960,* ARS 23-11, April 1961, Tables 4 and 9.

[2] Richard G. Axt, *The Federal Government and Financing Higher Education,* Columbia University Press, 1952, p. 207.

stations than at others, but Congress did not empower the Department of Agriculture to evaluate these differences or to allocate funds on the basis of past or prospective performance. In this respect, the pattern of federal support for research in agriculture is different from that which has grown up in other fields of study.

There are two exceptions to the formula distributions. Part of the federal appropriation is designated for regional research; that is, for projects involving the cooperation of two or more experiment stations. Proposals for the use of this money are submitted to an elected committee of nine experiment station directors who allocate the funds. This regional approach has proved so popular with the stations, that they have channeled an appreciable portion of their nonfederal funds into such projects. In addition, a lump sum for agricultural marketing research is allocated by the Department to finance what appear to be the most promising proposals submitted by the stations (and certain other groups) for such research.

Another feature of federal support for the experiment stations which differs from other federal research support is the large measure of discretion given the experiment station directors over the use of the funds. When a project is submitted for approval, an estimate of anticipated cost is given rather than a fixed budget. As long as the station director spends the money only in connection with approved projects and does not run over his total federal allotment for the fiscal year, he has considerable freedom in determining the amounts to be spent on various projects. Moreover, the federal funds can be used to cover almost any type of cost incurred in carrying out approved projects. They can be spent for salaries, animals, equipment, and supplies. Other uses include payments for a share of the utilities, janitorial service, and repairs on buildings used for federally approved projects, but federal funds cannot be used to pay rent on buildings owned by the college. Although the federal funds can also be used for the acquisition of land and buildings by the experiment stations, in practice, this seldom happens. Usually, the stations have applied federal funds to operating expenses and have relied on state sources for money to buy land and buildings.

Health and Military Research
before World War II

Prior to World War II, examples of federally financed research in colleges and universities, except for agriculture, were few and far between. As far back as 1879, the short-lived National Board of Health made a series of small grants to university scientists to cover the costs of special studies in the health field. "When the board had spent all of $30,000 in this manner over a period of three years is was considered extravagant and was shortly abolished."[3] The precedent was revived in 1918, when Congress voted $285,000 for a special study of venereal diseases—the first really substantial federal appropriation for medical research. At least part of this money was used to finance research by scientists working in universities.

The establishment of the National Cancer Institute in 1937 marked the beginning of a more permanent program of federal grants for health research in medical schools and other nonfederal institutions. From the beginning, the Cancer Institute not only operated its own laboratories, but undertook to stimulate and support related non-government research by means of training programs, fellowships, and grants-in-aid, many of them to university scientists. In the Institute's first three years of operations (1938-40), it awarded 33 grants totaling $220,000.[4]

The military services, before 1940, made very little use of the research resources of universities. The many Civil War innovations in military technology came from within the services and from private inventors who swarmed to Washington hoping to sell the government their designs for new weapons and other materiel. It fact, little scientific research was going on in the classically oriented American colleges of the day, and neither the military services nor scientists themselves had begun to think in terms of applying systematic scientific methods to the solution of military problems. Even the process of testing new weapons was haphazard by modern standards, especially in the Army. As one observer put it: "A few

[3] Shryock, p. 44, in "Selected References" at the end of this chapter.
[4] *Ibid.*, p. 273.

shots [were] fired in the neighborhood of the factory [and], if chance favored them, the piece was immediately received and added to the diversified assortment which already existed in the Federal artillery." [5]

There was some evidence, however, of a more systematic approach to innovations. The Navy, in 1862, created a Permanent Commission composed mainly of civilian scientists who tested and evaluated innovations, although the Commission did not undertake to develop new weapons. The Civil War also saw the creation by Congress of the National Academy of Sciences, a self-perpetuating group of 50 distinguished scientists who were to be available on request to render scientific advice to the government. However, the government made very little use of the Academy during the Civil War, and the Academy itself did not have resources with which to undertake research.

By the outbreak of the first World War, the importance of scientific research to military technology had become more obvious. In 1916, the National Academy of Sciences offered its services to the President in the national emergency. Wilson accepted, and a National Research Council was formed, composed of Academy members and other distinguished scientists. The object was to mobilize the research resources of the country—academic, industrial, and governmental—in the services of national defense. The National Research Council was initially financed by private foundations (and reverted to this status after the War), but it also received federal funds during the period of hostilities. Some grants were awarded to universities for defense-related research, but there was no substantial flow of federal funds to support military projects in civilian institutions. Acting mainly as a clearinghouse for scientific information and personnel, in most instances the Council simply put the services in touch with civilian scientists, who were then given direct commissions and assigned to work on research projects in military laboratories. Even the eminent physicist, R. A. Millikan, principal executive officer of the National Research Council and chairman of its physics committee, went about his duties in Army uniform.

The National Advisory Committee for Aeronautics (NACA) was

[5] Comte de Paris, quoted in Duprée, p. 121, as cited in "Selected References."

another federal agency which financed some university research. This Committee was created by Congress in 1915 to organize and supervise a federal research program in the new field of aviation. It conducted most of its research at Langley Field, Virginia, and other federal installations, but it also utilized university facilities. In fact, its first project involved a grant—all of $800—to the Massachusetts Institute of Technology in 1915. Larger grants were made later, especially in the 1930's. In 1939, the NACA had contracts for 12 special studies at 10 different universities.

The next national emergency, the Depression of the 1930's, produced a long list of proposals for federally financed research in colleges and universities, but little action. In 1933, Roosevelt appointed a Science Advisory Board under the chairmanship of physicist Karl T. Compton. The Board outlined a "Recovery Program of Science Progress" involving large federal expenditures on research in the natural sciences. The program was designed to give a scientific basis for conservation projects, public works planning, and the creation of new industries—utilizing university research facilities wherever possible.

At least three different programs were drawn up by the Science Advisory Board, the most ambitious calling for federal expenditures of $15 million a year for five years on scientific and engineering research. A third of this money was to be used to support research outside government laboratories. Nothing came of this, nor of a more modest proposal which followed it. However, the Works Progress Administration (WPA) did use some of its funds to pay unemployed scientists and technicians to work as research assistants on projects sponsored by tax-supported colleges and universities and directed by their faculty members. Almost every state university had at least one research project of this type in the late 1930's.

Despite these isolated examples, however, federal participation in nonagricultural research in universities before World War II may be described as negligible. Almost all of the approximately $15 million spent by the federal government for research in colleges and universities in 1940 was controlled by the Department of Agriculture. World War II was to change this picture.

The Growth of Research
During World War II

World War II, as Vannevar Bush has pointed out, was "the first war in human history to be affected decisively by weapons unknown at the outbreak of hostilities." [6] It was not immediately apparent that this would be so. In 1936, when the United States—belatedly realizing that another war was not entirely out of the question— began to take steps in the direction of rearmament, one of the first things the Army did was to cut its modest budget for research and development. "The amount of funds allocated to Research and Development in former years is in excess of the proper proportion for the item in consideration of the rearmament program," announced the Army General Staff. [7] The assumption was that, if war came, it would be fought with weapons already developed, and that taking the time and resources to develop new ones was a luxury inappropriate to a real crisis.

By the time the United States actually became involved in the hostilities, however, it was clear that this was to be no quick war fought with the weapons at hand. At best, it was going to be a long struggle against a strong and scientifically minded enemy, and the main hope for shortening the conflict lay in mobilizing scientific resources in a crash program to devise and develop radically new instruments of destruction and defense.

The World War II research effort was massive and all-inclusive. By the War's end, most of the nation's research scientists and scientific research institutions had been involved in projects which were financed directly or indirectly by the federal government. At least $3 billion was spent on research and development from 1941 through 1945, over 80 per cent of it by the federal government, according to the President's Scientific Research Board. [8] This does not sound like a staggering sum by current standards—even allowing for inflation—but it represented a major increase over prewar spending and a drastic shift in the position of the federal gov-

---

[6] As quoted in Stewart, p. ix; cited in "Selected References" for this chapter.
[7] Quoted in Duprée, op. cit., p. 367.
[8] See Vol. I, p. 11, of its report cited in "Selected References."

ernment, which probably had not been responsible for more than 15 per cent of combined public and private expenditures for research and development in the 1930's.

Some of the research was conducted in government laboratories, both existing and new ones, by staffs of scientists partially recruited from universities and industry. To this extent, the World War I precedent was followed, although on a larger scale and, in general, without actually putting civilian scientists into uniform. In addition, however, the government contracted with universities, industrial firms, and other institutions to conduct a substantial proportion of the research program in their own laboratories.

The government-financed research was aimed at winning the War, but not all of it was handled by the military services. In fact, by 1940, it was apparent that the military establishment had not been in sufficiently close touch with many recent scientific developments to be able to envisage their translation into new weapons. The scientists had to show the military what the possibilities were.

Accordingly, in 1940, the President created the National Defense Research Committee (NDRC) headed by the distinguished civilian scientist, Vannevar Bush. Bush was made directly responsible to the President and given wide and flexible powers for mobilizing scientific resources for war. Among his few specific instructions was that directing him to look into "the possible relationship to national defense of recent discoveries in the field of atomistics, notably the fission of uranium." A year later, NDRC and a parallel committee on medical research were brought together under the new Office of Scientific Research and Development (OSRD), also headed by Bush. At its first meeting, the NDRC made a decision which was to have lasting consequences for American universities. It decided not to set up its own laboratories, but to work through contracts, using existing facilities wherever possible. This policy was continued by OSRD.

Some of the War's most imaginative applications of scientific knowledge to military technology were made under NDRC-OSRD auspices, including the proximity fuse and the atomic bomb (transferred to the Army Corps of Engineers when it reached the development stage). Some of the projects were suggested by the military services, and some were initiated within OSRD—occasionally over the opposition of the military. In addition, the military services and the National Advisory Committee for Aeronautics had major research and development programs of their own, many of which involved contracts with universities.

The OSRD made an inventory of existing research facilities and personnel, with primary emphasis on universities. In selecting contractors, consideration was given to their ability to perform high-quality work in the shortest possible time, preferably with minimum interruption of their educational functions and with the minimum construction of new facilities. In some cases, however, it was necessary to construct a whole new installation, perhaps at some distance from the campus of the contracting institution, and to bring in large numbers of new staff. The Radiation Laboratory at Massachusetts Institute of Technology, OSRD's largest project, at one time had about 4,000 employees. The necessity for speed led to the concentration of research contracts in a small number of large institutions, such as MIT, the University of California, and the University of Chicago, with well-established research capabilities. Although OSRD was sensitive to criticism on this score, it was reluctant to risk the loss of time which might have resulted from turning over major projects to smaller or less experienced institutions.

In general, OSRD initiated the negotiations, approaching the institution considered most capable of undertaking a new project and requesting its cooperation. By the end of the War, however, the Medical Research Committee was relying on the institutions themselves to initiate projects by submitting "proposals for contract" which could be accepted or rejected by OSRD.

Certain problems arose in connection with the wartime research contracts which, two decades later, are still plaguing government-university relationships. One was the payment of faculty salaries. At first, OSRD did not pay the universities for the time spent on government research by regular faculty members during the academic year. When active hostilities began, however, enrollment and student fees dropped sharply, and OSRD found it necessary to relieve the universities of the burden of paying salaries to professors who increasingly were spending less time on teaching and more time on OSRD research.

A second problem was that of indirect or overhead costs. In addition to the direct costs of salaries, supplies, and equipment, OSRD agreed to reimburse the universities for the indirect costs of its projects, including the use of university buildings and the services of administrative staff. These indirect costs are always hard to measure, and it proved difficult—as it is still proving difficult—to find a formula which satisfied both the universities and the government. Typically, OSRD allowed 50 per cent of the salary budget of a project for overhead.

No one seems to know how much government money was spent on university research during World War II, except that it was large by prewar standards. In fiscal year 1944, OSRD alone made contracts with universities totaling $90 million, and OSRD was only one of several government agencies making such contracts. The $90 million (with some allowance for inflation) may be contrasted with the estimated total of $28 million spent by universities on all research in the natural sciences in 1938.[9]

Postwar Health and Defense Research

Some of the main features of the wartime research effort have persisted since the end of World War II. The federal government has continued to play an important role in research and development, financing approximately 60 per cent of the nation's research and development budget, as contrasted with about 80 per cent during the War and 15 per cent of the much smaller prewar budget.[10] Universities still conduct a significant portion of the research financed by the government, although the importance of the universities is not immediately apparent if one looks at the total federal budget for research and development. As Table I shows, only about 10 per cent of the estimated federal obligations for research and development in fiscal years 1959 and 1960 was for work to be per-

[9] Bush, p. 81, as cited in "Selected References."

[10] The President's Scientific Research Board, *op. cit.*, Vol. I, p. 10; and Dexter M. Keezer, "The Outlook for Expenditures on Research and Development During the Next Decade," *American Economic Review*, May 1960, p. 361.

formed by educational institutions. The reason this percentage is so small is that the "development" part of research and development is by far the most expensive, and most of it is performed for the government by private industry. In the research part, especially basic research, the universities' share is considerably larger.

TABLE I. *Federal Obligations for Research and Development, By Performer, Fiscal Years 1959 and 1960*

(In millions)

Obligations by Performers [a]	1959		1960	
	All R. and D.	Basic Research	All R. and D.	Basic Research
Federal installations	$1,729	$220	$1,842	$225
Profit organizations	4,399	44	5,102	106
Educational institutions . .	617	229	846	328
Proper [b]	(356)	(166)	(464)	(218)
Research centers [b]	(261)	(63)	(382)	(110)
Other	189	50	232	88
Total federal obligations . .	$6,934	$543	$8,022	$747

SOURCE: U. S. National Science Foundation, *Federal Funds for Science,* Vol. IX, 1960, pp. 52-55, 77-78.

[a] Note that these are obligations, not expenditures.

[b] "Proper" refers to the universities' regular laboratories; the "research centers" are separate facilities managed by the universities.

Since it is difficult to draw a firm line between basic and applied research or between applied research and development, the classification of particular projects into these three categories is often arbitrary. However, it appears that universities in 1959 and 1960 accounted for over 40 per cent of federal funds for work classified as basic research—that is, for fundamental scientific investigation aimed at the increase of knowledge. University obligations for both the applied research in which knowledge is applied to a practical objective, and development, in which new products and materials are designed and tested, account for much smaller portions of the total federal obligations in each classification.

A substantial portion of the government-sponsored research and development in universities is conducted outside the universities' regular laboratories in the research centers which are a legacy of World War II. In 1958, there were 28 federal research centers at 18 institutions. These university-managed nonprofit corporations, established for the purpose of doing government-financed research in installations built and owned by the government, vary considerably. Some are part of the campus of the managing institution and some are located at a considerable distance from it. One of the largest is the Los Alamos Scientific Laboratory in New Mexico, managed by the University of California. Many others also are large, even by comparison with the large universities with which they are associated. Lincoln Laboratories of the Massachusetts Institute of Technology, for example, has a budget larger than the MIT budget for teaching students. Eight research centers spent over $10 million dollars in fiscal year 1958.[11]

The research centers handle projects which are difficult to integrate into normal university activities. Approximately three-quarters of the expenditures of the research centers in 1958 was for applied research and development, not ordinarily performed by academic scientists, as contrasted with one-quarter of the expenditures of federal research funds by regular college and university departments.[12] Especially where military research requires special security precautions, it has often seemed desirable to set up a separate center. However, the work of the research centers is not confined to military research. Argonne Cancer Hospital and the National Radio Astronomy Observatory are examples of centers devoted primarily to nonmilitary basic research.

Military and Scientific Research

It is not always easy to distinguish military from nonmilitary research. Fundamental scientific discoveries frequently turn out to have unexpected military implications, and even the specific application of scientific knowledge to military problems may have

[11] U. S. National Science Foundation, *Reviews of Data on Research and Development*, No. 23, October 1960, p. 3.
[12] *Ibid.*, p. 1.

important nonmilitary by-products. Radar, rockets, and atomic energy all have civilian as well as military uses. Nevertheless, by any definition, federal support of research at universities since World War II has had a heavy military emphasis. The military services and the Atomic Energy Commission (AEC) combined have accounted for a very large share of the federal money going to universities for research, and most of the research they support is fairly closely related to national security problems.

This military emphasis, however, has declined somewhat in recent years. As may be seen in Table II, nearly 90 per cent of all federal funds for research in universities in 1952 came either from the Defense Department or the AEC. Even excluding the research centers, these two agencies still accounted for 76 per cent of the federal research funds going to colleges and universities proper in that year. By 1960, however, the combined share of Defense and AEC had dropped to 63 per cent when the research centers are included and to 44 per cent when they are excluded. The share of the National Science Foundation (NSF), on the other hand, increased substantially in this period, and an important new civilian agency was added—the National Aeronautics and Space Administration (NASA), successor to the National Advisory Committee for Aeronautics.

The National Science Foundation was an outgrowth of World War II, albeit a belated one. At the end of the War, the Office of Scientific Research and Development was disbanded, although some of its projects were taken over by other agencies. Vannevar Bush and other scientists, reluctant to leave federal support of science primarily to the military, immediately began to press for the creation of a permanent civilian agency to finance basic research in science through grants-in-aid to universities and to increase the supply of trained scientists through scholarships and fellowships. Bush's proposals, embodied in his report, *Science, the Endless Frontier*,[13] called for the creation of a National Research Foundation, to be run by a part-time board of scientists appointed by the President. This board was to choose the Foundation's executive director and to control the distribution of grants to universities for research.

[13] Cited in "Selected References for Chapter 3."

A different point of view was represented by Senator Kilgore who was reluctant to accord the scientists such a large measure of control over research funds. He introduced a bill calling for a more conventional government agency, to be headed by a presidentially appointed director, assisted by a board of scientists who would

TABLE II. *Federal Obligations for Research in Universities, By Agency, Fiscal Years 1952 and 1960* [a]

(Dollars in millions)

Agency	Including Research Centers				Excluding Research Centers			
	1952 [b]		1960 [c]		1952 [d]		1960 [c]	
	Amount	%	Amount	%	Amount	%	Amount	%
Defense . .	$156	53	$261	31	$100	74	$162	35
AEC	105	36	268	32	2	2	42	9
HEW	14	5	155	18	14	10	156	33
Agriculture .	13	4	31	3	13	9	31	7
NSF	1	0	60	7	1	1	60	13
NASA	0	0	64	8	0	0	8	2
All other . .	5	2	6	1	5	4	6	1
Total	$295	100	$846	100	$136	100	$464	100

[a] Note that these are obligations only, not expenditures.
[b] U. S. National Science Foundation, *Federal Funds for Science,* I, 1953, p. 41.
[c] *Ibid.,* IX, pp. 54-55.
[d] Kidd, p. 46, as cited in "Selected References for Chapter 3."

render advice, but not make decisions. These and other issues provoked a lengthy debate culminating in the establishment of the National Science Foundation in 1950. That government support of basic research did not entirely lapse for the duration of this debate is largely to the credit of the Navy. The Office of Naval Research in this period began a continuing program of support for basic scientific research in universities, which was much less closely tied to military applications than the programs of other services.

Administratively, NSF is a compromise between the Bush and Kilgore plans—it has a director appointed by the President, but decisions with respect to grants and fellowships must be ratified by a board of scientists.[14] More fundamentally, it represents a compromise between two points of view. One is that of persons advocating federal support of science centralized in a single agency, perhaps a Department of Science, with responsibility for formulating and carrying out a consistent national policy. Others would prefer that separate agencies be allowed to support whatever research seems relevant to their specific objectives. The National Science Foundation has supported basic research in universities on a comparatively modest, but expanding, scale. It has not supplanted other agencies—in fact, it has encouraged more generous support of basic research by other branches of the government. Nor has it undertaken to formulate or enforce a coordinated research policy for the government as a whole.

Health and Medical Research

Another postwar development has been the rapid expansion of government support for health research in the universities. From 1952 to 1960, as Table II shows, the share of total federal funds for research in the universities obligated to the Department of Health, Education and Welfare (HEW) increased from 5 to 18 per cent. Most of this support has been channeled through the National Institutes of Health (NIH) which is part of the Public Health Service. There are seven National Institutes—Cancer, Heart, Mental Health, Arthritis and Metabolic Diseases, Neurological Diseases and Blindness, Allergy and Infectious Diseases, and Dental Research—with separate research and training programs loosely coordinated by a central NIH director.

Congress has been generous with its support for medical studies; in fact, these National Institutes are among the very few agencies of the federal government which sometimes receive larger congressional appropriations than they request. The total NIH appropria-

14 Recent amendments to the National Science Foundation Act allow the Board to delegate this authority to the director and executive committee in certain cases where it seems advisable to speed project approval.

tions for research have grown 20 to 30 per cent per year since 1947—from about $8 million in 1947 to about $285 million in 1960.[15]

Following the tradition started by the National Cancer Institute before the War, a large portion of NIH research resources has been devoted to "extramural" programs—that is, to grants to universities, hospitals, and nonprofit research organizations. As Table III shows, colleges and universities (principally medical schools and graduate departments of biological science) have received over 70 per cent of the growing volume of NIH research grants in recent years.

TABLE III. *National Institutes of Health Research Grants, 1957-60* (Dollars in millions)

Year	Total Grants	Grants to Colleges and Universities	
		Amount	Per Cent of Total
1957	$ 82.5	$ 60.0	72.7
1958	99.5	72.8	73.2
1959	142.6	103.2	72.4
1960	198.7	140.3	70.6

SOURCE: Resources Analysis Section, Office of Program Planning, National Institutes of Health.

Purchase and Support of University Research

The federal government plays two roles with respect to university research. It purchases the research needed to carry out the operating responsibilities of the national government, and it supports research on the grounds that the increase of knowledge is itself in the national interest.

[15] For a good summary of the development of NIH programs, see Herbert H. Rosenberg, "Research Planning and Program Development in the National Institutes of Health: The Experience of a Relatively New and Growing Agency," *Annals of the American Academy of Political and Social Sciences*, January 1960, p. 104.

To a large extent, the military services regard themselves as purchasers, not supporters, of university research. Their major responsibility is national defense, and they turn to universities for help in solving defense-related problems when this seems to be the most advantageous way to get the job done. Often, they formulate problems themselves, and then begin contract negotiations with institutions which seem likely to be able to perform the work.

The National Science Foundation and the National Institutes of Health, on the other hand, have as their avowed objectives the support of research in the interest of the nation as a whole, and the strengthening of research capabilities of educational institutions. They allow the institutions to draw up their own projects and submit requests for support which are evaluated by advisory panels of scientists. The available funds are then allocated to those projects which seem to have the greatest scientific merit.

In practice, the distinction between the purchase and support of research is often blurred. The military services, realizing that advances in fundamental knowledge must precede military applications, have devoted some of their resources to supporting basic research. And in supporting basic research at universities, they behave very much like the National Science Foundation; university scientists formulate their own projects and the services support those which seem most promising. The Office of Naval Research took the lead in this direction immediately after the War. Its counterparts in the Army and the Air Force now are also supporting such research. The Atomic Energy Commission also invites proposals from universities for basic research projects to be supported with AEC funds.

It is often difficult to say where an idea for a research project originated. Informal conversations between the scientists and scientific administrators in and out of government usually precede the drafting of a formal agreement. A university scientist with an idea for a research project will "sound out" the government agency on an informal basis and may modify his project in accordance with the response he gets. Or an agency official may mention to university scientists that there is a need for research of a particular type and the agency would be receptive to proposals. This informal communication may be hard to detect in the language of the formal document which finally results. For example, when the Office of Naval Research decides to support a basic research project at a university it draws up a "task order" which reads as though the Navy had formulated the whole project and then asked the university to do it.

Scientific advisory committees are important in keeping the channels of communication open between the government and the universities. Almost every scientific agency of the government has one or more such committees on which university scientists usually are heavily represented. In some cases, they simply give advice; in others (for example, the National Science Foundation and the National Institutes of Health), they have real power in evaluating research proposals and deciding on the distribution of funds.[16]

To some extent, the distinction between purchase and support of research has been reflected in the distinction between contracts and grants. The AEC and the military services have usually employed the contract as a legal instrument, while NSF and NIH have used the grant to support research. In theory, a grant is simply a gift and need not imply any obligations on the part of the recipient. He may use the money as he sees fit and keep title to any property purchased with it. A contract, on the other hand, requires specific performance by both parties and usually spells out in considerable detail exactly what services are to be rendered by one party in return for payment by the other. Since the Constitution states that government property cannot be given away except by act of Congress, agencies which do not have specific authority to make grants must use the contract form.

Here again, however, a clear theoretical distinction has become blurred in practice. The difference between grants and contracts for basic research has not proved very marked. Grant instruments are usually somewhat simpler documents, which allow the investigator more freedom to deviate from his original proposal if he so desires. Both NSF and NIH emphasize that the recipient of a grant is free to conduct his project in whatever manner seems to hold the

---

[16] For an interesting discussion of the advisory committee system see Kidd, chapter 11, as cited in "Selected References."

most promise of yielding interesting scientific results. Perhaps somewhat plaintively, NSF does ask that it be kept informed of major changes of plans:

> The Foundation has no desire to inhibit the intellectual curiosity and research initiative of the principal investigator; however, on such occasions when either new and promising leads or fruitless lines of inquiry do occur, which may lead to major deviations from original research objectives, the Foundation would appreciate being informed of such deviations.[17]

However, no agency can give away public funds without any strings at all, and even the simplest grant instruments include descriptions of what is expected of the recipient, especially with respect to accounting and reporting procedures. The grant is usually paid in installments, and the balance may be withheld if the requirements are not met.

Contracts tend to be more complicated documents which place more specific obligations on the researcher, but this need not be carried to excess. The Office of Naval Research and certain other agencies have managed to employ the contract form without unduly limiting the freedom of the investigator to alter his research plans as the need arises.

The National Science Foundation not only adopted the grant form in supporting basic research in universities, but pressed Congress to allow other agencies to do the same. Accordingly, in September 1958, the 85th Congress passed Public Law 934, which gives any agency with the authority to support research the additional authority to use grants instead of contracts in its dealings with nonprofit institutions. This law also gives such agencies discretionary authority to vest in a nonprofit institution the title to any equipment purchased either under a research grant or a research contract, thus eliminating one of the practical differences between grants and contracts.

Until passage of Public Law 934, the Defense Department, among other agencies, had been obliged to use contracts in all cases. Subsequently, in August 1959, the Defense Department issued a direc-

---

[17] U. S. National Science Foundation, *Grants for Scientific Research*, January 1960, p. 12.

tive stating that the military services would henceforth be encouraged to use the grant form in supporting certain types of basic research—especially where it seems desirable to support a broad area of science, rather than the solution of a specific problem, and to minimize the administrative complications. Not much use was made of this authority until fiscal year 1961, and it is still too soon to say whether the shift from contracts to grants will make any significant difference in the nature of basic research support by the Defense Department.

Construction and Expansion of Research Facilities

In addition to supporting specific research projects, both the National Science Foundation and the National Institutes of Health have recently begun making grants for the construction and expansion of general-purpose research facilities at educational institutions. This is a rather new feature of government-university relations. Before World War II, permanent facilities were frequently excluded from the purposes for which government research money could be spent. During World War II, when research facilities and specialized equipment were constructed or expanded at many universities, the federal research contracts made it clear that these facilities were not to be given to the universities after the War. Real property was to be returned to its original condition at government expense unless the institution was willing to pay a negotiated amount for the improvements. All movable items were to be returned to the government. However, much of this equipment was later declared government "surplus" and turned over to the institutions for research use.

In the postwar period, some Atomic Energy Commission and Defense Department research contracts covered permanent additions to the facilities of the contracting institutions. And some grants for construction of research facilities at universities were made by the National Cancer and Heart Institutes between 1948 and 1952. However, the first general legislation to provide explicitly for government financing of research facilities as an end in itself was the Health Research Facilities Act of 1956. This set up a program of grants to nonprofit institutions for the construction and expansion of laboratories and other research facilities in the health sciences. Congress appropriated $90 million for the first three years, and a National Advisory Council on Health Facilities was formed to evaluate requests from institutions and advise the Surgeon General on the distribution of the funds. In 1958, Congress extended the program for another three years with appropriations continuing at $30 million a year.

The National Science Foundation in fiscal year 1960 started a similar program of matched grants to universities for the construction of graduate-level research laboratories in engineering and the natural sciences. Grants of over $2 million to 54 colleges and universities were announced by NSF for fiscal year 1961. Also, NSF has financed the construction of certain specialized and expensive research equipment for the joint use of groups of universities. An example is the big radio telescope at Green Bank, West Virginia.

Impact of Federal Research on Colleges and Universities

Federal funds for research have become a major item in the consolidated income statement of higher educational institutions, as may be seen in Table IV. In recent years, colleges and universities have derived 12 to 14 per cent of their combined educational and general income from federal research funds with an additional 5 to 6 per cent coming from other federal sources. In 1939-40, only about 7 per cent of their educational and general income came from any federal source.

These figures could easily be misinterpreted. They definitely do not indicate that the average higher educational institution (if there is such a thing) derives 14 per cent of its income from federal research. These funds are concentrated in a relatively small number of universities and technological schools with strong graduate departments in the natural sciences. Most colleges have no federal research projects at all.

Distribution of Research Funds Among Institutions

In 1957-58, there were about 1,900 colleges and universities in the United States, including junior colleges. Only 363 of these reported any separately budgeted expenditures for research and development in that year. This does not mean that the other institutions did no research at all—some of their faculty members undoubtedly put time on small projects financed out of their regular departmental budgets. However, they did not receive outside support for these

TABLE IV. *Percentage Distribution of Educational and General Income of Colleges and Universities, by Source*

Source	1939-40	1953-54	1955-56	1957-58
Student fees	35.2	23.5	25.2	25.0
State and local government.	30.7	35.6	34.6	34.2
Federal government	6.8	17.8	17.1	18.9
Research	(n.a.)	(12.0)	(12.3)	(14.2)
Other	(n.a.)	(5.8)	(4.8)	(4.7)
All other sources	27.3	23.0	23.0	21.9
Total	100.0	100.0	100.0	100.0

SOURCE: U. S. Office of Education: *Biennial Survey of Education* and *Higher Education,* March 1960, p. 10.

activities or budget their own funds specifically for research. Within the group which did report research expenditures, moreover, the distribution of both federal and nonfederal funds was far from even. Approximately half the federal money was spent by research centers at 18 institutions. Of the federal research funds going to colleges and universities proper (excluding research centers and agricultural experiment stations), as Table V shows, about half went to 14 institutions and nearly three-quarters to 36 institutions.

The degree of concentration in federal research funds seems to have dropped somewhat between 1953-54 and 1957-58. The National Science Foundation, however, suggests that this change may be partly due to a shift of federal research projects from regular departments (especially engineering schools) in large universities to research centers.

Concentration in a relatively small number of institutions is not peculiar to federally sponsored research. It is characteristic of university research in general, and is closely associated with the similar concentration in graduate enrollment and graduate degrees. Data are available for 20 institutions in 1953-54 and 1957-58 which illustrate this point. The 20 institutions (excluding research centers and experiment stations) which spent the most federal money for re-

TABLE V. *Concentration of Federal Research Funds in Colleges and Universities, 1953-54 and 1957-58*

Number of Institutions	Per Cent of Federal Funds	
	1953-54	1957-58
Largest 6	33	28
Largest 14	56	49
Largest 36	81	73

SOURCE: U. S. National Science Foundation, Office of Special Studies.
NOTE: Data exclude research centers and agricultural experiment stations.

search in 1953-54 spent 66 per cent of the total. They also spent 55 per cent of the nonfederal funds for separately budgeted research and development. In 1957-58, these same 20 institutions spent 54 per cent of the federal money and 51 per cent of the nonfederal.[18] They also awarded 52 per cent of the doctorates in science and 54 per cent of the doctorates in science and social science combined.

The concentration of research funds and graduate students in a few institutions is not new; in fact, it was probably more pronounced in the 1930's than now. The federal government might have radically altered the existing pattern during World War II had it consciously sought to build up research facilities in new places, but, in order to get quick results, it chose not to do so. This concentration has con-

[18] U. S. National Science Foundation, Office of Special Studies.

tinued in the postwar period, and has tended to become self-perpetuating. Research funds, both public and private, are attracted to
institutions with strong graduate departments, and able faculty and
graduate students are attracted by the availability of research funds.

Not only is federal research money concentrated in a small number
of institutions, but almost all of these institutions, except for those in
California, are located in the northeastern and north central sections
of the country. This fact has not escaped the notice of congressmen
from other areas, and it has aroused some concern among educators.
Part of the debate on the National Science Foundation was on a
proposal that NSF be required to distribute part or all of its funds
on a geographic basis in hopes of building strong research institutions in all sections of the country. Most scientists opposed this on
the grounds that money turned over to relatively weak institutions
might be wasted, and no such provision was passed. Both NSF and
the National Institutes of Health have attempted to encourage the
development of research capacity in new places, but the dozen or so
institutions which have received the bulk of the military research
money are also high on the list of recipients of NSF and NIH
grants.[19] Twenty institutions received 54 per cent of the NIH research grant funds in 1960. This proportion had dropped only three
percentage points since 1957, despite an increase from 209 colleges
and universities receiving NIH funds in 1957 to 293 in 1960.[20]

Distribution of Research Among Fields of Study

The national interest in military and medical problems has meant
that almost all federal research funds going to universities have been
concentrated in the physical and biological sciences, and it is these
departments in the universities that have felt the primary impact
of the federal programs. Table VI shows estimates of the total
amounts spent by universities on separately budgeted research in
the sciences in 1957-58 and the sources of these funds by fields of
study.

The federal government financed over two-thirds of all the

[19] Kidd, *op. cit.*, p. 55.
[20] National Institutes of Health, Office of Program Planning, Resources Analysis Section.

separately budgeted scientific research conducted in universities in 1957-58 (even excluding research centers and experiment stations). The proportion of research financed by the government was extremely high in the physical sciences, high in engineering, somewhat less in the life sciences, and even smaller in the social sciences. The proportion of federally financed university research in the sciences seems to have remained fairly stable in the last few years. An

TABLE VI. *Separately Budgeted Scientific Research and Development in Colleges and Universities, by Fields, 1957-58*

(Dollars in millions)

Field	Including Research Centers and Experiment Stations		Excluding Research Centers and Experiment Stations	
	Total	Federally Financed	Total	Federally Financed
Engineering	$186.4	85%	$ 66.1	66%
Physical sciences	262.3	90	98.6	80
Life sciences	251.5	50	139.5	62
Social sciences	35.6	48	23.4	38
Total	$735.8	73%	$327.5	67%

SOURCE: U.S. National Science Foundation, *Reviews of Data on Research and Development,* No. 19, April 1960, pp. 4, 6.

earlier NSF survey indicated that 69 per cent of all separately budgeted research in colleges and universities proper (excluding research centers and experiment stations) was federally financed in 1953-54 as compared with 67 per cent four years later. Within the total, the federal share rose somewhat in the life sciences in this period, but dropped in engineering.

The National Science Foundation estimated that the cost to the universities of unbudgeted "departmental research" in 1953-54 was roughly a fifth of the cost of all separately budgeted research. If this proportion is still approximately correct, the addition of departmental research to the figures given in Table VI would bring total research expenditures of colleges and universities (including experiment stations and research centers) in 1957-58 to something like $880 million, about 60 per cent financed by the federal government. The federal share would be smaller in all fields if departmental research were included, and considerably smaller in the social sciences.

No one knows, of course, what would have happened to the distribution of research funds in the postwar period in the absence of the federal research programs. Professors in the social sciences and the humanities sometimes bemoan the concentration of federal funds in the natural sciences and the "imbalance" that this creates in university life. The situation has certainly been hard on the morale of those in the nonscientific fields, but the availability of federal funds in the sciences actually may have given the universities more freedom to devote nonfederal resources to research in other fields.

Undesignated Grants

One persistent criticism of the federal research program in universities is that it has been primarily project-oriented. The government has a long tradition of financing specific research projects, rather than giving block grants to be used at the discretion of the college or university doing the research. It has been alleged that the project system transfers control of the directions which inquiries should take from the institutions to the government agency which approves and disapproves projects. Also, it is felt that the project system tends to favor areas in which the research to be done can easily be divided into neat packages—at the expense of newer areas in which specific projects may be hard to define. Whatever the merits of this argument, the National Science Foundation has recently taken a step in the direction of undesignated grants. On May 28, 1960, NSF announced a new policy of granting to each institution a sum of money equal to 5 per cent of the NSF research grants it received in the previous year. The institution may spend this sum on strengthening its scientific departments in any way it sees fit.[21]

[21] New York Times, May 29, 1960, p. 1.

The funds need not be used for research, but can be applied to salaries or equipment or whatever the institution feels it needs. This program, which was expected to give the institutions about $3 million in free funds in fiscal year 1961, will do nothing to alter the concentration of federal money in science and in large institutions, but it is a significant step away from the time-honored project approach.

Even more recently, the National Institutes of Health announced a program of institutional grants to begin in fiscal year 1962. The NIH has legislative authority to use up to 15 per cent of its total extramural research funds for institutional grants and has devised an elaborate formula for apportioning the money. Part of it will be distributed in equal shares to all recognized medical, dental, osteopathic, and public health schools. A second part will be distributed among these schools and graduate departments of biological science in proportion to the total federal funds for medical research they are currently receiving. A third part will be distributed in proportion to the nonfederal support they are receiving for medical research. This last provision is supposed to give the institutions an incentive to raise funds from other sources.

Even within its regular extramural program, moreover, NIH has been moving consciously toward larger and longer-term grants for broadly defined projects. Sometimes this has been accomplished by consolidating several specific projects at the same institution under a larger and more generally stated grant. About a quarter of NIH grants are for amounts over $100,000, and projects of this size tend to be stated in rather general terms which give the investigators considerable freedom. Lengthening the term of the grant—some NIH grants are for as long as seven years—is also expected to give the investigators more freedom to pursue promising lines of work without the necessity of producing immediate results in order to justify continued support.

Computation of Overhead Costs

A heated debate has raged over the question of whether the government should be required to pay the full cost of all the research it finances or whether the universities should sometimes contribute. The main issue is whether—in addition to paying direct costs of equipment, materials, salaries of research assistants, and so forth—the government should be obliged to compensate the universities fully for the indirect costs reasonably attributable to government-financed projects. It is always difficult to arrive at a formula for allocating these overhead costs. If a government research project is housed in a university building which is also used for other purposes, it is hard to say exactly what part of the cost of heating, maintaining, and depreciating the building may reasonably be attributed to the research project. If the dean or the purchasing agent or the university counsel spends time over the administrative details of a research contract, it is not clear what part of his salary should be charged to the contract—especially since the university would have to pay his salary in any case. Nevertheless, these indirect costs are real costs, and a university (or a business) which took on a very large volume of government research without asking for payment of indirect costs would soon find itself in serious financial difficulty. All of this, of course, is an old story to accountants, who are accustomed to devising rules of thumb, however arbitrary, for allocating overhead costs.

There is no real argument about the principle of full overhead cost payments in connection with the research centers or with most of the military contracts. The armed services usually purchase research services from universities on terms somewhat similar to those purchased from industry, except that industry is allowed a profit margin and universities are not. The arguments here have been largely over different formula for computing the full cost, not over whether or not it should be paid. Even with respect to basic research contracts, the services have accepted the principle of full-cost payments.

The National Science Foundation and the National Institutes of Health, on the other hand, not only have regarded themselves as supporters, not purchasers, of research, but also they have been so regarded by Congress. The universities come to these agencies with research ideas and ask for financial support. Presumably, these are basic research projects which the universities would finance themselves if they had the resources. An institution which objects to absorbing part of the overhead need not apply for the grant. Following this rationale, Congress has limited NIH to the payment of a relatively small allowance for overhead (recently 15 per cent of direct costs), which does not compensate the universities for the full costs which could reasonably be attributed to NIH projects.

The National Science Foundation, although not specifically limited by its own legislation, has not adopted a full-cost policy with respect to its own grants—probably for fear of disapproval by Congress and the Bureau of the Budget. From 1951 through 1959, although NSF was pressing Congress to allow all agencies to pay full overhead costs, recipients of its own grants were limited to an overhead allowance of 15 per cent of direct costs. This percentage, however, was raised to 20 per cent for NSF grants on January 1, 1960.

An attempt has been made at NSF to estimate the actual indirect costs attributable to all separately budgeted research, conducted by colleges and universities in 1957-58, by applying the so-called "Blue Book Formula" used by the armed services in computing overhead costs—a formula generally accepted by the universities as a fair one. Computed on this basis, indirect costs averaged about 28 per cent of direct costs in 1957-58. The federal agencies sponsoring university research collectively paid only about two-thirds of the indirect costs which the Blue Book Formula would have called for, leaving the institutions to absorb the other third (about $16.7 million dollars).[22] Some other observers have put the university contribution even higher.

Compensation for Research by Faculty Members

Another much-debated question is whether federal funds should be used to pay the salaries of regular faculty members working on federal research projects. Some institutions have taken the stand that no regular faculty members should receive compensation from the government for the time spent on sponsored research. These institutions fear that a professor, part or all of whose salary was being paid by an outside organization, might begin to consider

[22] U. S. National Science Foundation, *Reviews of Data on Research and Development*, No. 19, April 1960, p. 7. The Blue Book has since been supplanted by a new formula contained in Budget Bureau Circular A-21, September 10, 1958, revised January 7, 1961.

himself an employee of that organization. His loyalty and sense of belonging to the university community might be impaired, and freedom to express his own views or to report scientific results inimical to the interests of the sponsor might be in jeopardy. Other universities have taken these dangers less seriously. They have felt that sponsored research should pay its own way, rather than drain the resources of the university. Hence, the time which faculty members take away from their teaching and other university duties for work on sponsored research should be fully chargeable to the sponsor.

Government policy has evolved in the direction of paying reasonable compensation for faculty time spent on federal research projects, except where institutional policy is opposed. As we have seen, the Office of Scientific Research and Development encountered the problem during World War II. At the very beginning OSRD refused to pay salaries to tenure faculty members, but this policy soon proved too hard on the institutions and OSRD was compelled to revise it. The military services, in general, have considered compensation for faculty time a legitimate cost of the research performed for them by universities, and the National Institutes of Health now takes the same position. The NIH policy statement on this matter reads as follows:

> In accordance with the policy of the grantee institution, grant funds may be used to provide regular salaries in whole or in part, including summer salaries, of professional personnel . . . in proportion to the time spent directly on the project being supported. Grant funds are not intended to relieve the grantee institution of its normal responsibility for salaries.[23]

The National Science Foundation for some time took the position that it did not "encourage the subsidization of tenure faculty salaries during the academic year by means of grant funds," although it would pay some salaries under certain circumstances. This statement was revised in June 1960, to read as follows:

[23] U. S. Department of Health, Education and Welfare, Public Health Service, *Grant and Award Programs of the Public Health Service*, I, 1959, p. 8.

As a general policy, the Foundation recognizes that salaries of tenured and non-tenured faculty members and other personnel associated directly with the research constitute appropriate direct costs, in proportion to the time to be spent on the research. Funds may be requested accordingly. . . . Grant funds may NOT be used to augment the total salary or rate of salary of faculty members of institutions of higher education during the period of time covered by the term of faculty appointment.[24]

Employment of Graduate Students

A large number of graduate students are employed as research assistants on federally sponsored research projects in universities. Rough estimates prepared by the Bureau of the Budget indicate that there were 20,000 to 30,000 of these research assistants in fiscal year 1960, and about 40,000 may be expected for fiscal 1962.[25] In 1953-54, when a thorough study of the support of graduate students was made by the National Science Foundation, approximately a quarter of the full-time graduate students in physics and chemistry and a third of those in engineering held federal research assistantships. In that year, the median earnings of federal research assistants were about $1,600, and undoubtedly have risen substantially since then.[26]

Some of these students would find other sources of support, particularly teaching assistantships, if the federal research jobs were not available. In fact, many universities have found it very difficult to get enough well-qualified graduate students to help with undergraduate teaching in the sciences, in part because the best students prefer to take fellowships or research assistantships. Nevertheless, it seems likely that the existence of jobs for graduate students on federal research projects tends to increase the number of graduate students in the sciences. These jobs also influence choices of special fields within the sciences. A student often uses work performed on

[24] U. S. National Science Foundation, *Grants for Scientific Research,* January 1960, p. 6, as amended June 1960.

[25] Kidd, *op. cit.,* p. 129, and U. S. Bureau of the Budget, *Special Analysis of Federal Research and Development Programs in the 1962 Budget,* January 1961.

[26] Kidd, *op. cit.,* p. 130, based on U. S. National Science Foundation, *Graduate Student Enrollment and Support in American Universities and Colleges, 1954,* 1957.

a federal project as the basis for a doctoral dissertation and goes on to become a specialist in the same area. The availability of research jobs probably contributes to the concentration of science graduate students in a few major institutions with large amounts of federal research money, although the converse is also true. Universities tend to seek and obtain government contracts when they can show that they have a pool of graduate students to help carry out the work.

To What Extent is Research Support Aid to Higher Education?

The arguments about overhead costs and payment of faculty salaries reflect a basic difference in points of view on the purpose of federal support of research. Some persons regard government-financed research in universities as a form of federal aid to higher education, supporting one of the traditional functions of the universities. Others regard it primarily as a service performed by the universities for the government, often to the detriment of regular teaching functions.

There are certainly great differences in the extent to which the various types of projects financed by the federal government can be regarded as part of the traditional activities of educational institutions. On one end of a continuous scale, one might place a small grant to an individual faculty member to support some basic research in which he is interested. The professor thought of the project and applied for money to support it. He would have gone ahead with the project, even in the absence of government support, if he could have obtained the necessary funds from his university or from a private source. The government pays the direct expenses of the project plus some allowance to the university for overhead. It does not pay any part of the professor's salary, since he continues to carry a full teaching load at the university, but he can use a portion of the money to employ one or two graduate students as part-time research assistants.

Farther along this scale might be a contract between a university and one of the military services for basic research deemed to have some ultimate defense application. The project is directed by a faculty member who, although regularly paid by the university, may draw a salary from the project during the summer months, or when temporarily relieved of part of his teaching duties. Several other faculty members are associated with the project, and a dozen or so graduate students are employed part time in the winter and full time in the summer. In addition, several research associates may have been brought in specially to work on the project. They become full-time employees of the university, but their salaries are paid from the government funds, and they have no teaching responsibilities and no permanent status on the faculty. The original idea behind the project may have come from the military, or it may have come from faculty members who thought of research problems which seemed both interesting in themselves and likely to be of interest to the military. Needed equipment and apparatus are financed by the government, but housed in university buildings. The government pays all the direct costs of the project, plus an allowance for overhead.

Another step along this scale would be a research center, housed in a separate building, probably owned by the government, but situated on or near the university campus. This nonprofit corporation managed by the university may have several contracts at once, perhaps with different branches of the government. The center may have a full-time director and quite a few full-time staff members, but graduate students and university faculty also work there. The latter may receive compensation as consultants or as part-time or temporary staff members.

Finally, at the far end of the scale is the major research center built by the government on government land, and located at some distance from the campus of the university which manages it. Most of the center's personnel work full time, and have no real connection with the university. Faculty from the managing university may serve as consultants or as summer staff, but so may scientists from other institutions.

It seems clear that federal funds spent on these major research centers do not constitute federal support of higher education in any meaningful sense. It happens that federal expenditures on the project at Los Alamos show up as income in the budget of the University of California, and are transferred from there to the consolidated income statement of higher educational institutions as "income from the federal government." Rather anomalously, federal expenditures on the Brookhaven National Laboratory on Long Island do not show up in the budget of any educational institution, since Brookhaven is managed by a group of institutions which have formed a joint corporation known as Associated Universities. One might argue that any federal support of research redounds to the ultimate benefit of universities, but it would be very hard to argue that federal support of Los Alamos is support of higher education, while support of other federal laboratories, including Brookhaven, is not. Los Alamos cooperates with educational institutions on research problems and provides summer and leave-of-absence employment for university scientists, but so do other government laboratories. They also compete with universities for full-time scientific personnel. If the management of government research centers of the Los Alamos type were suddenly transferred to nonprofit corporations not connected with individual universities, the federal contribution to the income of higher educational institutions would appear to drop by many millions of dollars, but the effect on higher education would be very hard to detect.

Government expenditures for research centers located on university campuses probably should not be regarded as support for higher education either, although here the case is a little less clear. The managing university may well benefit from having the research center on its campus. In particular, the possibility of part-time employment at the research center and of intellectual interchange with the center's staff may attract better faculty and better graduate students to the university.[27]

The case becomes still less clear, as we move to government-financed research performed by regular faculty members within the university itself. In many ways, the university as a whole benefits from this type of federal research support. Many faculty members

[27] Russell Thackrey, of the American Association of Land-Grant Colleges and State Universities, has pointed out that locating a national park near a university would attract better faculty members, too, but would not ordinarily be regarded as federal aid to higher education.

are so eager to do research that they would leave the university and go elsewhere if research funds were not available. To be sure, some might be happy to work on less expensive projects if funds were less abundant. But the existence of the government money often relieves the university of having to chose between finding more funds of its own to support research and losing some of its ablest professors. Moreover, students, especially graduate students, benefit not only from the part-time employment, but also from the stimulation of the research atmosphere.

Nevertheless, heavy involvement of regular faculty members with federal research is not without costs, both to the university and to the students. Even where the government undertakes to compensate the university for the full indirect costs associated with individual research projects, some administrative and other costs of a large volume of government research still may not be fully compensated. Moreover, although the government may pay a portion of a faculty member's salary in order to compensate the university for the time he takes away from teaching to devote to government research, the portion may be unrealistically small. Some of the faculty members with government research projects spend most of their time on research and the administrative and fund-raising activities associated with sponsored research to the neglect of their students, especially their undergraduate students. This is not the fault of the government, but is a by-product of the existence of federal research money.

In summary, perhaps the most that can be said is that the substantial share of federal funds now going to support research centers in universities cannot be regarded as federal support for the teaching functions of higher educational institutions. With respect to the rest of federal funds, many questions might be raised, but much of the support benefits the recipient institutions and enables them better to perform their teaching functions. However, since federal research funds are highly concentrated in a few large universities, the federal support actually may increase the difficulties of nonrecipient institutions. They may find it more difficult and expensive to maintain a good faculty and a stimulating atmosphere than if the federal research money were being spent entirely outside the academic market place—or not at all.

SELECTED REFERENCES FOR CHAPTER 3

1) Donald K. Price, *Government and Science,* New York University Press, 1954.
2) A. Hunter Duprée, *Science in the Federal Government,* Harvard University Press, 1957.
3) Richard H. Shryock, *American Medical Research, Past and Present,* The Commonwealth Fund, 1947.
4) Irvin Stewart, *Organizing Scientific Research for War,* Little, Brown and Co., 1948.
5) The President's Scientific Research Board, *Science and Public Policy* (six volumes), 1947.
6) Vannevar Bush, *Science, The Endless Frontier,* Government Printing Office, 1945.
7) *Annals of the American Academy of Political and Social Science,* January 1960. Entire issue devoted to "Perspectives on Government and Science."
8) Charles V. Kidd, *American Universities and Federal Research,* Belknap Press, 1959.
9) National Science Foundation, *Federal Financial Support of Physical Facilities and Major Equipment for the Conduct of Scientific Research,* June 1957.
10) ———, *Government-University Relationships in Federally Sponsored Scientific Research and Development* (NSF 58-10), 1958.
11) ———, *Basic Research, A National Resource* (NSF 57-35), 1957.

4

Federal Assistance
to Students

DIRECT FEDERAL PAYMENTS to students, unlike the federal
grants to institutions of higher education, are of rather recent origin
in the United States. There are a number of ways in which students
can be aided. Three important ways are through scholarships, loans,
and the provision of part-time employment. In the past 25 years,
the federal government has experimented with all three. Other traditional forms of aid are the remission of tuition at federal institutions and the Reserve Officer Training Corps program, both of
which are discussed in chapter 6.

Until the postwar period, the federal government's aid to students
was mainly restricted to emergency needs or military training.
During the Depression of the 1930's, a federally supported student
work program was one of the emergency relief measures. During
World War II, college students—mainly in scientific fields where
manpower was short—received war loans to complete their training.

Since World War II, there has been a marked change in federal
policy related to students. The government is now heavily involved
in supporting undergraduate and graduate students, as well as
postdoctoral and faculty fellows. First, there was the GI Bill of
Rights, under which about 3.5 million veterans received training
in institutions of higher education (almost 10.5 million, in all types
of educational benefits). Then, in 1958, passage of the National
Defense Education Act opened up opportunities under which over
100,000 undergraduates and graduate students have received loans

61

for college work and about 3,000 students hold fellowships in education, the humanities, the sciences, and foreign languages. During this period, other federal agencies also established fellowships and other special arrangements to train increasing numbers of scientists. The National Science Foundation (NSF) has about 4,000 full-time and part-time fellowships; the National Institutes of Health (NIH), about 3,700; and the Atomic Energy Commission (AEC), 200 fellowships, all of them full-time.

The outlook for meeting crucial national needs for highly qualified manpower is improved by the large numbers of full-time graduate students included in the figures given above. Something like 6,600 predoctoral students held full-time federal fellowships in 1960-61, all but about 2,000 of them in the sciences. The total includes 2,500 National Defense fellows; about 2,400 NSF fellows; about 1,000 NIH fellows; plus the AEC fellows. Furthermore, the 6,600 figure not only excludes faculty and postdoctoral fellows, but also medical students and a very large number of NIH trainees, some of whom are graduate students in the health sciences.

Admitted, 6,600 is not a very large proportion of a total graduate student enrollment of about 305,000—or even of an estimated full-time enrollment of 115,000.[1] However, most graduate students never get doctorates. Many never wanted to, others flunk out or change their plans. The federal fellowships are intended almost entirely for a small group of students who might be called "serious qualified doctoral candidates."

Currently, a little less than 10,000 doctorates are awarded annually. It probably takes the average graduate student from five to six years to get his degree.[2] This implies a pipeline of roughly 50,000 to 60,000 students at any one time who will actually win their degrees. Approximately 10 to 15 per cent of this number holds full-time federal fellowships. But in the sciences, alone, at least 20 to 25 per cent of the "serious qualified doctoral candidates" probably hold federal fellowships. Moreover, a large proportion of the doctoral candidates in the sciences, who do not have fellowships, sup-

[1] U. S. Office of Education, Circular No. 625, June 1960. Figures are for the academic year 1959-60 and would be slightly higher for 1960-61.

[2] Bernard Berelson, *Graduate Education in the United States*, McGraw-Hill, 1960, p. 158.

port themselves by working as research assistants under federal research contracts and grants to universities, as do many candidates for other degrees.

Student Aid During the Depression and World War II

In the depths of the Depression, with a quarter of the labor force out of work, young people whose unemployed parents could no longer support them were leaving schools and colleges, and themselves swelling the ranks of the unemployed. The college student work program was designed to help some of these young people continue their education while earning money in useful part-time jobs on the campus.

The program, started by the Federal Emergency Relief Administration in late 1933, aided an average of 100,000 students a month in the school year 1934-35. It was then taken over by the National Youth Administration, which administered the program until its termination in 1943. All nonprofit tax-exempt institutions of higher education were eligible to participate and almost all of them did. Each institution was told how many students it might employ under the program—the quotas being based on a percentage of regular enrollment. The payments were made directly to the students, but each institution was responsible for selecting students to participate in the program (on the basis of need), finding somthing for them to do, and forwarding records of the number of hours they worked to the National Youth Administration.

Undergraduates were not allowed to earn more than $20 a month, nor graduate students more than $40, but these amounts made it possible for many students to stay in college who otherwise would have had to leave. It was estimated that over 600,000 students participated in the program between 1935 and 1943. Applications at most institutions were many times the allowed quotas, especially in the early days of the Depression. The main difficulty was finding enough genuinely useful work for the students to do, since it was one of the stipulations of the program that the student workers might not replace any of the institution's regular employees. Some students were assigned "busy work" which benefited neither the institutions nor themselves, but many more did useful jobs in return for their modest stipends.

The student war loans program, started during World War II, was designed to encourage students who were within two years of graduation in such vital fields as engineering, physics, chemistry, medicine, dentistry, and pharmacy to finish their education before going to work. A student in one of these fields was allowed to borrow up to $500 a year at 2.5 per cent interest if he agreed to complete his course of study and accept war-related employment on graduation. Between 1942 and 1944, a little over $3 million was loaned to about 11,000 students—most in medicine and engineering. For the most part, they proved to be good credit risks.[3] Although the circumstances under which this program was enacted were special, the program provides an interesting precedent for federally financed student loans.

The GI Bill of Rights

By far the most extensive venture into government aid for students in our history was the program of educational benefits for veterans which began with the Servicemen's Readjustment Act of 1944—the "GI Bill of Rights." The GI Bill was a new concept in veterans legislation. Veterans of previous wars had received substantial benefits from the federal government in cash and in land, and disabled veterans had received hospital care and special pensions. After World War I, it was decided that both the veterans and the government would benefit if a major effort were made to retrain disabled soldiers for useful jobs in civilian life, rather than having them live the rest of their days in government hospitals. An extensive vocational rehabilitation program for disabled veterans was undertaken, partly in federal hospitals and partly in regular schools, colleges, and universities. Disabled veterans authorized

---

[3] George E. Van Dyke, "Government Experience with the Student War Loan Program," *Higher Education*, November 15, 1949, pp. 61-63.

to attend civilian institutions received a monthly stipend to cover living expenses, and the federal government paid tuition and fees on their behalf to the institution. Nothing was done to train or educate those who had been lucky enough to get through the war without injury.

As World War II drew to a close, there was a great deal of discussion of what to do for returning veterans. It was generally agreed that the government should do everything possible to retrain and rehabilitate the disabled, but there also was special concern about the readjustment problems of ablebodied servicemen. Would men whose education had been interrupted by four or more years of military service return to schools and colleges for the training needed for jobs in the postwar economy? And if they did not, would the economy be able to absorb several million more workers, who would flood the labor market even before reconversion was complete? Out of this discussion came the educational provisions of the GI Bill.

There were four basic pieces of legislation covering educational benefits for veterans:

1) Public Law 16 (78th Congress) provided vocational rehabilitation and training for disabled veterans of World War II.
2) Public Law 894 (81st Congress) extended similar benefits to disabled veterans of the Korean War.
3) Public Law 346 (78th Congress), as amended, provided educational and training allowances for all World War II veterans for periods up to 48 months, depending on length of service.
4) Public Law 550 (82nd Congress) extended similar benefits to Korean veterans for periods up to 36 months.

Children of servicemen killed in war or in extra-hazardous peacetime service were also awarded educational allowances. Repeated efforts to extend educational benefits to veterans of peacetime service have failed in Congress.

The original purpose of the GI program was to compensate veterans whose education had been delayed or interrupted by the War. Public Law 346 stated that persons not over 25 years old when they entered the service would be presumed to have had their education delayed or interrupted, but that those who were over 25 would have to demonstrate such delay or interruption. These requirements were eliminated by early amendments to the legislation, however, and all veterans who had served more than 90 days were made eligible for the educational benefits, no matter how old they were or what they had been doing, or planning to do, when they entered the service.

Eligibility for the benefits depended exclusively on military service—not on aptitude for education. A presidential committee (the Osborn Committee), appointed at the end of 1942 to study postwar educational benefits, recommended that all eligible veterans be given one year's training and that only a limited number, selected for their "special aptitudes," be aided for a longer period. This suggestion was approved by President Roosevelt and embodied in a bill reported favorably by the Senate Committee on Education and Labor. Congress as a whole, however, rejected the idea of aptitude tests. Senator Pepper reflected a widespread sentiment when he suggested that there was something undemocratic about such tests:

> . . . while I understand thoroughly what the Germans have always done about segregating those who are qualified for higher education from the masses who are destined for manual work and that sort of thing, at the same time it looks to me like any boy or girl who wants to go to college and who is able to make creditable grades, if they go there, should be entitled to go without some board somewhere getting this fellow into a laboratory, as it were, and deciding what potentialities are within him.[4]

The legislation finally enacted provided educational allowances for any veteran who could obtain admittance and maintain passing grades in any school, college, or university recognized by his state or by the Veterans Administration (VA). The length of time for which he could draw the benefits depended entirely on the duration of his military service. Thus, the educational benefits of the GI Bill were the twentieth century equivalent of "forty acres and a mule." They gave the returning serviceman, not a cash bonus,

---

[4] Quoted in report of the U. S. President's Commission on Veterans' Benefits, p. 5, as cited in "Selected References" at the end of this chapter.

but some intangible capital, which, if he had the ability and the inclination to use it, could increase his future earning capacity.

The benefits for veterans applied to all kinds and levels of education. They could be used to finish high school, to learn radio repair or tap dancing, to do graduate work in philosophy, or to "study" French on the Riviera. Over 10 million former servicemen

TABLE VII. *Veterans Utilizing Various Types of Educational Benefits*

(In thousands)

Type	Vocational Rehabilitation		Education and Training		Total [a]
	World War II	Korean War	World War II	Korean War	
Institutions of higher education ..	152	22	2,200	1,166	3,435
Schools below college level	149	26	3,500	824	4,364
Apprentice, on-the-job and on-the-farm ..	312	14	2,100	312	2,656
Total	614	62	7,800	2,302	10,455

SOURCE: Bradford Morse, "The Veteran and His Education," *Higher Education*, March 1960.

[a] Less than the sum of the columns because some veterans (about 3 per cent) pursued courses under more than one program.

have already taken advantage of the programs, and some are still eligible to do so. As may be seen in Table VII, only about a third of the total number have used their benefits to attend institutions of higher education.

The World War II GI program is essentially over. It reached a peak in 1947-48 when over a million veterans were enrolled in colleges and universities, constituting about half of total enrollment. Thereafter, the number began to drop off. The Veterans Administration reported that in November 1960, there were less than a hundred veterans taking vocational or educational training at any level under the World War II legislation. The number of Korean veterans in colleges and universities dropped from a peak of about 482,000 in November 1956 to about 168,000 in November 1960, and is expected to fall off rapidly in the next year or so. The number of war orphans drawing educational benefits is still increasing, since many of these children were born in the early 1940's and are just now reaching college age. About 8,000 war orphans drew allowances for college level study in 1959-60.

Under the World War II legislation, the college-going veteran received a monthly "subsistence" allowance which varied with the number of his dependents. The Veterans Administration also paid to the college he was attending the "customary" tuition, fees, and other charges paid by other students up to a limit of $500 for each academic year. This last provision worked to the disadvantage of public institutions, whose tuition and fees are customarily low and represent only a small part of the actual cost of educating a student. For this reason, state institutions which usually charged higher fees to out-of-state students were allowed to treat all veterans as nonresidents. When an institution was still not satisfied (or, in a few cases, when the VA thought the nonresident fee was too high), it could negotiate with the VA for payments based on the actual "cost of teaching personnel and supplies." These negotiations caused severe administrative headaches and considerable friction between the colleges and the VA.

Partly because of these administrative difficulties and the feeling that some colleges had raised tuition fees in order to profit from the program, government payments to institutions were entirely dropped when the GI Bill was extended to the Korean War veterans in 1952. The Korean veterans received flat monthly payments (adjusted to number of dependents) which were somewhat higher than the earlier subsistence payments, but they were required personally to pay tuition and all other fees. This simplified the administration of the program considerably, although it presumably tended to induce veterans to choose institutions that cost less than the ones they might have chosen under the earlier system.

No real evaluation of the GI Bill has yet been made, but the program at the college level is generally regarded as a success. Certainly, many veterans—no one knows exactly how many— would have gone to college anyway, but at least a substantial minority would have been unable to attend if they had not had the federal benefits.[5] As a group, the veterans performed at least as well in college as nonveterans and prewar students, and often better.

The immediate impact on the colleges of returning veterans of World War II was tremendous. Male enrollment, which had already regained its prewar level by 1945-46, jumped from 928,000 in that year to 1,836,000 in 1947-48, almost all of the increase being accounted for by returning veterans.[6] Instructors, classrooms, and housing had to be found for this influx almost overnight. College construction had virtually ceased during the war, construction materials were still in short supply, and almost all institutions experienced severe overcrowding. Part, but only part, of the pressure was relieved by government gifts and sales to the colleges of prefabricated barracks and other surplus military buildings and equipment.

As Table VIII shows, government payments to colleges and universities for veterans' tuition and fees reached about $365 million in 1947-48 and then tapered off. The subsistence allowances paid to World War II veterans do not show up in this table, nor do any of the payments made under the Korean program, since the latter went directly to the veterans themselves, not to the institutions. At the peak of the World War II program, slightly more than half of the total veterans' payments went to private institutions, which obtained 29 per cent of their educational and general income from this source, as contrasted with 20 per cent for all public institutions.

---

[5] In one study of veterans in college, about 10 per cent of the students interviewed said they definitely would not have gone to college without the GI Bill benefits. Another 10 per cent said they "probably" would not have gone. Norman Frederiksen and W. B. Schrader, *Adjustment to College: A Study of 10,000 Veteran and Nonveteran Students in Sixteen American Colleges,* Princeton, Educational Testing Service, 1951, p. 34.

[6] U. S. Office of Education estimates of regular session enrollment.

TABLE VIII. *Federal Payments to Institutions of Higher Education for Veterans' Tuition and Fees*

(Dollars in thousands)

Payments	1945-46	1947-48	1949-50	1951-52	1953-54
Federal payments to institutions for veterans' tuition and fees.....	$61,164	$364,727	$307,325	$146,900	$44,368
As a per cent of all student fees	22	54	44	25	7
As a per cent of total educational and general income	7	24	17	7	2

SOURCE: U. S. Office of Education, *Biennial Survey of Education.*

Postwar Committees and Commissions on Higher Education

The postwar decade saw a great deal of national soul-searching and viewing-with-alarm, some of it directed toward higher education. There were committees and commissions and reports and proposals, but relatively little action—at least at the federal level.

In 1946, President Truman appointed a distinguished Commission on Higher Education, under the chairmanship of George F. Zook. In its lengthy report,[7] the Zook commission estimated that about half of all American young people had the ability to complete 14 years of schooling and that about a third could complete "an advanced liberal or specialized professional education" involving four or more years of college training. The fact that many able students were dropping out of school, for financial and other reasons, before completing this much education was regarded by the Commission as a waste of human resources resulting in serious loss both to the individuals and to the nation.

The Zook Commission recommended that state and local governments provide free public education through the fourteenth grade

[7] See report of U. S. President's Commission on Higher Education cited in "Selected References."

in both junior (two-year) and senior colleges, and that they reduce all other tuition and fees charged by public institutions to the levels prevailing in 1939. To help the states with this program, the Commission proposed federal grants-in-aid to the states, both for operating expenses of public institutions and for capital outlays. In addition, the Commission recommended a substantial federal scholarship program designed to prevent able students from dropping out of school for financial reasons.

Under this plan, scholarships would be provided for 20 per cent of all nonveteran college students. They would be awarded by state scholarship commissions, but the recipients would be allowed to go to any college to which they could gain admittance, in or out of their home states. The amount of each scholarship would depend on the student's need, but the Commission suggested an average of $400 per year (maximum $800), renewable for as long as seven years.

The Commission also recommended federal fellowships for graduate students, paying $1,500 a year and awarded on the basis of competitive examination. The graduate program was to start with 10,000 fellowships and build up to 30,000 a year. The holder of the fellowship was to choose his own field of study and his own university. An initial federal appropriation of $135 million was recommended to finance the first year of the scholarship and fellowship program. The cost would have risen, however, to around $400 million a year by 1960 (even if the size of individual scholarships had remained the same), as the GI Bill tapered off and as larger numbers of young people entered the college-age group.

The Zook report aroused much discussion both in educational and in legislative circles, but it did not result in any comprehensive legislation. Some existing federal programs were expanded in this period, the GI Bill was extended to Korean veterans, some graduate fellowships for specialized types of study were established by the National Science Foundation and other scientific agencies (discussed further below), but no general program of federal scholarships or fellowships was adopted.

Ten years later, in 1956, President Eisenhower appointed an equally distinguished Committee on Education Beyond the High

School, under the chairmanship of Devereux C. Josephs, to look into the situation again and make recommendations. The Josephs Committee was concerned about many of the same problems that were stressed by the Zook Commission. These included the need to increase the supply of college teachers and the desirability of reducing the number of students who drop out of school before getting the education their abilities warrant. Like the Zook Commission, this Committee estimated that about half of American young people could profit from some education beyond high school. Its recommendations based on this estimate, however, were entirely different. Some of the noneconomic barriers to higher education, such as lack of information and motivation on the part of students, were emphasized, and the Committee urged the secondary schools to improve their guidance programs. It pointed out that more scholarships were needed and advocated greater reliance on student borrowing. But the Committee felt that nonfederal sources probably could be counted on for the needed increases in scholarship and loan funds. If any federal scholarship program were to be found necessary in the future, however, the Committee felt it should provide not only stipends for students, but also cost-of-education grants to the colleges attended, since the tuition paid by the student hardly ever covers the full cost to the institution of his education.

The only immediate federal action recommended by the Josephs Committee was an "experimental" work-study program, under which 25,000 to 50,000 college students would receive government compensation for work performed at the institutions they were attending. It also advocated that the federal income tax laws be amended "in ways which will permit deductions or credits on income tax returns by students, their parents or others who contribute to meeting the expenditures necessarily incurred in obtaining formal education beyond high school." [8]

The Josephs Committee issued its report in July 1957, and Secretary of Health, Education and Welfare Folsom appointed a Committee to study the recommendations and draw up legislative pro-

[8] See the *Second Report* of The President's Committee on Education Beyond the High School, p. 11, cited in "Selected References."

posals. About the same time, the House Committee on Education and Labor began a series of hearings in various parts of the country on possible federal scholarship and loan programs for college students. It seems doubtful, however, that any actual legislation would have resulted if the Russians had not launched their Sputnik in October.

This dramatic demonstration of technical prowess shocked both the country and the Congress, and turned the rather desultory debate on higher education into a burning national issue. Sputnik was widely assumed to indicate that Russian scientific education was superior to ours and that our system must be improved in the interests of national survival. Many people seemed to blame our failure to beat the Russians into space less on the low priority which the government had assigned to the space program than on the poor quality of algebra teaching in American high schools. In the next few weeks, dozens of bills were introduced in Congress calling for federal programs to strengthen American education, particularly scientific education, in the service of national defense.

The National Defense Education Act

When the House Committee on Education and Labor opened its scholarship and loan hearings in the summer of 1957 it had called first, as is customary, for the views of the Secretary of Health, Education and Welfare and the Commissioner of Education. When—three months after Sputnik—the corresponding Committee of the Senate opened similar hearings in January 1958, the professional educators took second place after the scientists. The first witness was Detlev Bronk, President of the National Academy of Sciences, who was followed by Lee DuBridge, I. I. Rabi, Wernher von Braun, and Edward Teller, all of whom were called upon to give their views on what was wrong with American education. The Senate Committee hearings went on for several weeks and the House Committee hearings were resumed. In all, nearly 4,000 pages of testimony were received from scientists, educators, government officials, and citizens, representing a wide spectrum of views on American education and what, if anything, should be done to improve it.

There was more agreement on problems than on policies. Dozens of witnesses stressed the small proportion of American high school students enrolled in science, mathematics, and language courses; the shortage of well-qualified secondary school teachers, especially in the foregoing subjects; the large number of high school graduates (200,000 a year was the most-quoted estimate) with the ability to go to college who were not going; and the shortage, present and expected, of people trained for college teaching and research, especially in the sciences.

Many witnesses advocated federal scholarship programs. One suggested 1,000 federal scholarships a year; another 400,000; but the most frequent proposals involved 10,000-50,000 federal scholarships annually, paying $500 to $1,000 each. Some thought the scholarships should be awarded on the basis of need; others that they should be essentially prizes given for achievement on tests or in high school, irrespective of financial need. Some thought earmarked scholarships should be used to attract students to the sciences; others that recipients should be free to study in any field. Still other witnesses expressed the view that scholarships destroyed individual initiative, and that loan and work-study programs were to be preferred since they encouraged self-reliance. Various types of tax relief for parents and students were also proposed. Some witnesses maintained that the main problem was not in the colleges, but in the high schools. Thus, they suggested federal aid to the states either for special programs to strengthen the teaching of science or languages, or high school guidance, or for more general support of primary and secondary education. Still others deplored any extension of federal aid to education at any level.

Out of this welter of proposals and counterproposals and after considerable deliberation, there emerged the National Defense Education Act, signed by President Eisenhower on September 2, 1958. It was a hodgepodge piece of legislation, representing deliberate compromises, and it was labeled an emergency defense measure, not a permanent program of federal aid to education as such. Among other things, the Act provided grants to states for laboratory equipment and other aids to science teaching in elementary and secondary schools; for guidance, counselling, and testing programs; for the improvement of language instruction; and for vocational training of scientific technicians. It is the college student loan and graduate fellowship provisions of the Act, however, which are of concern here.

The National Defense Student Loan Program

Undergraduate scholarships were eliminated in the course of floor debate in the House on the National Defense Education Act, but the legislation did provide for federal contributions to funds set up by institutions to make low-interest loans to needy students. The term "institution of higher education" was broadly defined to include almost any college or junior college giving at least two years of work acceptable for credit toward a bachelor's degree. Over 1,300 of the approximately 2,000 eligible institutions have participated so far.[9]

The government contributes 90 per cent of the capital of these student loan funds, while the institutions put in the remaining 10 per cent. The federal funds are distributed among the states on the basis of full-time enrollment in higher education. But, within each state, funds are distributed to participating institutions in proportion to their requests for them. This last provision was based on the assumption that the institutions themselves are the best judges of their students' needs. However, to prevent padding of requests when there are not enough funds to go around, the Commissioner of Education has worked out an informal system whereby institutions may be asked to scale down requests which seem unreasonably large in proportion to their enrollment. The law has placed a ceiling of $250,000 on the federal contributions to the loan fund at any single institution. In practice, this means that

[9] A small, but very influential, group of colleges has refused to take part in the program in protest against a provision of the Act which requires the student borrower not only to take an oath of loyalty to the United States, but also to sign an affidavit disclaiming disloyal associations and beliefs. Some others have felt their students did not need the funds or that the amounts to which they would have been entitled were too small to bother with.

the share of the largest institutions is less than it would be if the funds were distributed only in proportion to enrollment. The Kennedy Administration has recommended that the ceiling for a single institution be raised to $500,000, but, at the time this was written, Congress had not acted on the recommendation.

Both undergraduates and graduate students are eligible to borrow so long as they are full-time students in good standing and need the money to complete their studies. An individual student may borrow up to $1,000 a year, or $5,000 in total. The institutions make their own selections among applicants for the loans, but the Act provides that "special consideration shall be given to (A) students with a superior academic background who express a desire to teach in elementary or secondary schools, and (B) students whose academic background indicates a superior capacity or preparation in science, mathematics, engineering, or a modern foreign language." However, nothing is said about the courses these students shall pursue after they get the loans.

The loans bear interest at 3 per cent, beginning one year after the borrower ceases to be a full-time student at the institution. They are to be repaid in periodic installments over a 10-year period. Payments of both interest and principal may be suspended while the borrower continues full-time studies at another institution or serves in the armed forces. A student who borrowed to complete his undergraduate education, then spent three years in the Army and four years as a graduate student, would have been out of college seven years before he was obligated to make payments on his loan. As an inducement to students to go into teaching, the Act provides that part of the repayment obligation may be forgiven if the student becomes a teacher. In the language of the Act, an amount "not to exceed 50 percentum of any such loan (plus interest) shall be canceled for service as a full-time teacher in a public elementary or secondary school in a State, at the rate of 10 percentum of the amount of such loan plus interest thereon, which was unpaid on the first day of such service, for each complete academic year of such service."

The program did not really get under way during 1958-59. Most of the $30.5 million appropriated by Congress for that year did not become available until the end of the academic year. The unused funds were carried over to 1959-60, and about $40 million more was appropriated by Congress. At the end of June 1960, the loan fund amounted to $79.3 million of which $70.8 million had been contributed by the federal government. The balance consisted of contributions from the participating institutions and a small amount of interest.[10] By mid-1960, the participating colleges and universities had made or approved over 140,000 loans. Women, who constitute roughly a third of all students, constituted about a third of the borrowers. Graduate and professional students, who represent about 10 per cent of total enrollment, also represented about 10 per cent of the borrowers. The average size of loans climbed from a little over $330 in 1959 to nearly $500 in 1960, with graduate students borrowing somewhat more, on the average, than undergraduates. Men tended to borrow more than women, but the differences were slight. (See Table IX.)

It is too soon for a definitive evaluation of the student loan program. The eagerness of both students and colleges to participate in the program—except when they had qualms about the loyalty affidavit—has surprised those who thought it might take some time for loan financing of college expenses to become accepted. Of the 1,357 colleges which had participated in the program by June 1960, 639 had never before administered student loan funds. Moreover, the existence of the government program has stimulated colleges and other organizations and institutions to set up student loan funds of their own. The apparent willingness of women to borrow also has been a surprise to some observers. The forgiveness provisions for elementary and secondary school teachers, of course, make the program especially attractive to education students, most of whom are women. In fact, the terms are so attractive that anyone with reasonably certain expectations of going into teaching would be almost foolish not to apply for a loan. Approximately half of the loans approved in fiscal years 1959 and 1960 went to students who had been given "special consideration" because they expressed a desire to teach.

[10] A small proportion of the institutional contribution was borrowed from the government as permitted by the Act.

TABLE IX. *National Defense Student Loans Approved, By Sex, Level, and Average Amounts, Fiscal Years 1959 and 1960*

Sex and Level	Number [a]	Average Amounts
1959:		
Undergraduate men	14,958	$299
Undergraduate women	7,199	275
Graduate and professional men	2,359	379
Graduate and professional women	315	362
Total	24,831	$333
1960:		
Entering freshmen—men	16,707	$469
Entering freshmen—women	13,473	470
Other undergraduates—men	50,780	488
Other undergraduates—women	25,413	478
Graduate and professional men	11,103	617
Graduate and professional women	1,524	598
Total	119,000	$495

SOURCE: U. S. Office of Education, *The National Defense Student Loan Program: A Two-Year Report*, pp. 18-19, as cited in "Selected References for Chapter 4."

[a] Some of the 1960 students presumably borrowed in 1959 as well.

The National Defense Fellowships

The part of the National Defense Education Act providing for federally financed graduate fellowships had two objectives. The first was to increase the supply of trained college and university teachers; second was promotion of a wider geographical distribution of facilities for graduate study. Numerous witnesses at the hearings emphasized that undergraduate enrollments were likely to double between 1958 and 1970; and that the quality of college teachers—insofar as quality can be equated with the acquisition of higher degrees—would decline if immediate steps were not taken to increase the flow of students in and out of graduate schools. Others pointed out that graduate study was highly concentrated in a few institutions in a small number of states. They feared that the effect of increasing fellowships under which the recipient was allowed to choose his own place of study might simply be to overcrowd the "prestige" institutions, while potentially strong centers of graduate study in other parts of the country would remain underutilized.

Congress specified that the Commissioner of Education should award fellowships to students who had been accepted for study in particular graduate programs approved by the Office of Education at particular institutions. The programs approved were to be either "new or expanded" and were to "substantially further the objective of increasing the facilities available in the nation for the graduate training of college and university teachers and of promoting a wider geographical distribution of such facilities throughout the Nation." Moreover, applicants were to be given preference if they expressed an interest in going into college or university teaching.

The Act provided for 1,000 fellowships the first year and 1,500 in each of the three succeeding fiscal years. Since the followships run for three years, 4,500 students will be supported simultaneously at the height of the program. The fellows receive stipends of $2,000 for the first year; $2,200 for the second; $2,400 for the third year; plus $400 a year for each dependent. These amounts are supposed to be sufficient so that fellows can study full time, and they are not permitted to hold paying jobs during the academic year except for limited part-time research and teaching commitments at their institutions.

In addition to the stipends paid the fellows, the Act authorized the government to compensate the institutions for the added cost of the fellows' education. In the words of the Act:

There shall be paid to the institution of higher education at which each such person is pursuing his course of study such amount, not more than $2,500 per academic year, as is determined by the Commissioner to constitute that portion of the cost of the new graduate program or of the expansion in an existing graduate program in which such person is pursuing his course of study, which is reasonably attributable to him.

Although passage of the National Defense Education Act came

too late to set up fellowships for the academic year 1958-59, the Office of Education was immediately flooded with proposed programs for 1959-60. Altogether, 169 institutions in 46 states and Hawaii submitted over a thousand proposals for new or expanded graduate programs calling for around 6,000 fellowships. Applications came from nearly all the 160 institutions which awarded the Ph. D. degree in 1958 and from some which did not. Out of the applications, the Office of Education, assisted by an outside advisory committee, picked 272 programs involving 1,000 fellowships, the maximum authorized by the Act for the first year. More applications came in for 1960-61, out of which 204 new programs were picked. In addition to renewals, more fellowships were awarded to 200 of the programs established in the previous year. Altogether nearly 2,500 students held National Defense fellowships in 1960-61.

The Office of Education has interpreted a "new or expanded" graduate program to mean a program involving new faculty or facilities—not just a reshuffling of courses taught in the same place by the same people. In distributing the fellowships among fields of study, the Office has used the present distribution of faculty by fields as a rough measure of future demand, without attempting more elaborate projections of needs or shortages in specific areas. However, it has taken into account the support already provided in the sciences through research assistantships on federal contracts as well as fellowships administered by the National Science Foundation, National Institutes of Health, and other agencies. Thus, the Office of Education has tended to emphasize new programs in the humanities, education, and the social sciences—all areas in which there has hitherto been almost no federal activity. Even so, the natural sciences have by no means been left out of the fellowship program, as Table X shows.

In choosing particular programs to be supported, the Office of Education has had to balance the dual objectives of the Act— widening the geographic distribution of graduate facilities and increasing the supply of graduate teachers. Two states, New York and California, whose universities awarded the most doctorates in 1956-57, have also received the largest absolute number of National

Defense fellowships. But the relative impact of the program has been much greater in some of the southern and mountain states whose universities have given almost no earned doctorates in the past. For example, universities in five states (Idaho, Maine, South Dakota, Mississippi, and Montana) awarded a grand total of 3 earned doctorates in 1956-57, less than .05 per cent of the total. But these same states received 117 National Defense fellowships, 4 per cent of the total number, which presumably will increase

TABLE X. *Distribution of National Defense Fellowships, by Field of Study*

Field of Study	1959-60		1960-61	
	Number	Per Cent	Number	Per Cent
Humanities	248	25	408	27
Education	47	5	108	7
Social sciences	264	26	444	30
Biological sciences	158	16	147	10
Physical sciences	224	22	246	16
Engineering	59	6	147	10
Total	1,000	100	1,500	100

SOURCE: U. S. Office of Education, *Report on the National Defense Education Act, Fiscal Year Ending June 30, 1960,* p. 65, which is cited in "Selected References for Chapter 4."

their production of doctorates by several hundred per cent in the near future. By contrast, universities in five states (New York, California, Illinois, Massachusetts, and Pennsylvania) awarded 4,031 doctorates in 1956-57, or 46 per cent of the total number awarded. These same states received 593 National Defense fellowships for 1959-60 and 1960-61, or 24 per cent of the total.

Technically, the National Defense fellowships are awarded to individuals by the Commissioner of Education, but, in practice, the Commissioner has relied on the institutions to select the fellows from among the applicants. He has not attempted to ensure that awards made in different places go to students of comparable ability. Undoubtedly, some winners of the fellowships in universities with weak graduate departments are not as well qualified as some students who are refused fellowships at universities whose well-established graduate departments attract better applicants. The hope, of course, is that the fellowship programs will serve to strengthen the weak graduate programs and ultimately to attract better qualified students to these new centers of graduate study. Also the Office of Education has left to the institution the interpretation and application of the congressional directive that preference be given to students "interested in teaching in institutions of higher education." The kind of evidence of this interest which should be exacted from applicants has not been specified.

The one clause in the Act which has caused the most administrative difficulty has been that providing for cost-of-education payments to the institutions with approved graduate fellowship programs. The inclusion of this provision reflected recognition of the fact that educating a student, particularly a graduate student, always costs an institution far more than the student pays in tuition. Legislation which simply increased graduate enrollment without compensating the institutions for the added costs of the new graduate programs could have been more of a burden than a blessing to the colleges and universities involved.

The idea of cost-of-education payments was a good one, but unfortunately there is no obvious procedure for measuring the cost of educating a student, and cost accounting practices differ widely from institution to institution. The Act specifies that the payment shall cover that portion of the cost of the program in which a fellow is studying "which is reasonably attributable to him." This implies that the institutions should try to estimate the marginal cost of a graduate student; that is, the cost of adding one more student to a given program. In practice, it has been necessary to resort to estimates of average cost. The institutions have been asked to compute, if possible, the total cost of the "new or expanded" graduate program divided by the number of students in it. If accounting practices at the institution do not permit this, then the institution must estimate the per-student cost of instruction in the next largest unit for which separate records are kept—be it the department, the graduate school, or even the whole university. Since most of these estimates have exceeded $2,500, the maximum allowable under the Act, the actual cost-of-education payments have averaged just under $2,500.

A main criticism of the National Defense fellowship program has been its restriction to "new or expanded" graduate programs involving new staff or facilities. Many universities have pointed out that they would welcome additional qualified students in their existing graduate programs and would be able to teach these students at small additional cost. In fact, many departments at good, but not particularly prestigious, institutions have some graduate programs in which only a handful of students are enrolled. Some of these departments would be able to take on two or three times as many graduate students without appreciable increases in staff or facilities, and the expansion might be stimulating both to the faculty and to students who are already there. If the object of the federal legislation is to build strong graduate departments and to increase the production of college teachers, it would seem sensible to bring students into existing programs which are not being fully utilized before, or in addition to, building new ones.

It has also been pointed out that many graduate students start teaching in college before they have their doctorates. Almost every small college has some junior faculty members with what have been called "A.B.D. degrees" (all but the dissertation). They left graduate school, often for financial reasons, after completing all the requirements for a doctorate except the dissertation. Many accepted teaching appointments in hopes of writing theses in their spare time, but with heavy teaching loads the spare time never materializes. The Office of Education estimates that there are several thousand such "A.B.D.'s." Giving those who are qualified a year of subsidized study, in which to catch up with the new developments in their fields and complete their degree requirements, would be a help in raising the average quality of college faculty and inducing these people to stay in teaching.

With these objections in mind, the Kennedy Administration asked Congress to approve a number of amendments to the National Defense Education Act, some of which would affect the graduate program. The Administration's bill (H.R. 6774 and S. 1726, 87th Congress, 1st Session) would alter the graduate fellowship program as follows:

1) The fellowship program would be permanent and the number of new fellowships to be awarded annually in "new or expanded" programs would be increased from 1,500 to 2,500. With continued three-year fellowships, approximately 7,500 graduate students would be supported simultaneously under this phase of the federal program after 1964.

2) The award of 2,500 additional graduate fellowships would not be tied to "new or expanded" programs. These could be used to encourage college teachers without doctorates to get their degrees or, in some instances, to do postdoctorate work, and to attract students to existing graduate programs which seemed to be underutilized.

3) To reduce the complications involved in calculating the cost-of-education grants, the universities would be awarded a flat $2,500 for each fellowship holder in a new or expanded program and $2,000 for each fellowship holder in the other programs.

4) The Commissioner of Education would be authorized to replace fellows who died or resigned before the expiration of their fellowship terms.

There was no strong opposition to these amendments in Congress, but they were lost in the confused battle over aid to primary and secondary schools which took place in the first session of the 87th Congress. Just before it adjourned in September 1961, Congress extended the National Defense Education Act for two more years, but without any amendments. This means that the Commissioner of Education is authorized to continue awarding 1,500 fellowships a year in "new or expanded" programs.

National Defense Language Fellowships

In addition to the general graduate fellowship program just described, the National Defense Education Act authorized the award of another group of special fellowships for graduate study in important, but hitherto neglected, modern languages. As directed by the Act, the Commissioner of Education has selected 85 languages in which trained linguists are needed by government, business, or education, but in which the available instruction seemed to be inadequate. Arabic, Chinese, Hindi-Urdu, Japanese, Portugese, and Russian have been designated "first priority languages," but the complete list includes such exotic-sounding languages as Marathi, Telegu, Ilocano, Kanarese, Kpelle, Rajasthani, Tigrinya, and Yoruba.

Under this program during 1959-60, a total of 171 graduate students received stipends, and 472 language fellowships, including some renewals, were awarded for study in 1960-61. The stipends vary—a few of the language fellowships are for summer study only —but the maximum is $2,700 for the year, plus tuition, travel, and an allowance for dependents. The fellowship recipients are required to give "reasonable assurance" that they will be available either to teach the language or to perform other public service for which knowledge of the language is necessary when they have completed their studies. The government is not going to subsidize anyone who wants to study Tagalog purely for his own amusement.

Federal Fellowships to Train Scientists

The National Defense fellowships were the first under which graduate students could choose among all the traditional fields of graduate study, including the humanities and the social sciences; but they were by no means the first federal fellowships at the graduate level. At the end of World War II, the country experienced an acute shortage of well-trained young scientists in almost all fields. Universities were trying to hire new faculty members to help teach the flood of returning veterans, and were finding it hard to compete with the salaries and research opportunities offered young scientists at expanding government and industrial research laboratories. Not only had demand greatly increased since the prewar period—both for teachers and researchers—but also the supply had all but dried up, since very few students started graduate work during the War.

Federal support for graduate students in the health sciences had begun as early as 1938, when the National Cancer Institute offered its first fellowships, and such programs expanded rapidly after the War. Starting more slowly in the postwar period, the federal fellowship programs in the physical sciences have increased most rapidly in the post-Sputnik period.

Health Fellows, Trainees, and Training Grants

The organizations which together comprise the National Institutes of Health are primarily devoted to research related to the particular disease with which each is concerned—cancer, heart, mental, and so on—in NIH laboratories and in hospitals and universities receiving NIH support. The interest of the institutes in education as such has been the outgrowth of their interest in research. It stems from the realization that, in the long run, the progress of medical research depends on attracting many able and well-trained people into research careers.

At present, NIH offers half a dozen different types of fellowships. Research fellowships are awarded to predoctoral, postdoctoral, and special students in the "basic and clinical health sciences," which allow the recipient to spend full time on research, or training for research, for the duration of the fellowship. Most of these fellowships are for a year, but some are for longer periods, and the predoctoral fellowships are renewable as long as the fellow is making satisfactory progress toward his degree. The predoctoral fellowships carry stipends of $1,800, $2,000, and $2,200, plus dependency allowances, for the first year, the intermediate year, and the terminal year, respectively. The postdoctoral and special fellowships are more generous. Some "senior research fellowships" and "foreign research fellowships" are also awarded. Moreover, qualified students in medical and dental schools are encouraged to drop out of regular course work for a period of one, two, or three years to do scientific research on a "post-sophomore research fellowship" from NIH. In all, over 2,400 full-time fellowships were awarded by NIH in fiscal year 1960.

In addition to the full-time fellowships, about 1,200 part-time fellowships were awarded in 1960 for student research in schools of medicine, osteopathy, dentistry, public health, and nursing. These fellowships (worth $600 each, plus an allowance to the institution for indirect costs) are not awarded directly to the students by NIH. Rather, a certain number are allocated to each qualifying institution which requests them, and the institution is allowed to use the funds to compensate students for time spent on research—either part time during the regular term or full time for two or three months. The main aim is to orient the students toward

TABLE XI. *National Institutes of Health Fellowship Awards, By Type of Fellowship, Fiscal Years 1959 and 1960*

Type	1959	1960
Predoctoral	678	1,021
Postdoctoral	627	822
Special	124	202
Part-time	1,052	1,261
Post-sophomore	126	134
Senior	165	226
Foreign	51	57
Total	2,823	3,723

SOURCE: National Institutes of Health, Division of Research Grants.
NOTE: Includes renewals.

research while they are still in school in the hope of attracting them to research careers.

Another type of support provided by NIH is substantial "training grants" made to schools of medicine, dentistry, public health, and osteopathy, and to other university departments with graduate programs in the health and biological sciences. In general, these grants are used for two purposes. They pay operating expenses (including faculty salaries) of special programs designed to train students for research, teaching, or clinical work related to cancer, heart disease, mental health, and other specific health areas; and they pay stipends (traineeships) to students in these programs. The institutions are allowed to select the trainees and determine the level of stipends. These stipends of full-time trainees are generally sufficient to allow the trainee to devote himself to his training without support from other sources. The amount varies widely from program to program, since the trainees range from undergraduate student nurses to practicing psychiatrists giving up substantial incomes to return for additional training.

The exact number of students receiving stipends under the training grants program is not known, since NIH has not collected this information centrally. It has been estimated that about 10,000 trainees received full-time or part-time support under NIH training grants in fiscal 1959, representing the equivalent of about 7,000 full-time man-years. About three-fifths of these trainees were predoctoral students, and the rest were postdoctoral. In addition, a smaller number of traineeships are awarded directly to students for training in other specialized fields. The latter differ very little from fellowships.

The NIH training grants are of particular interest, not only because they provide support for students, but because they constitute direct federal subsidies to educational institutions to cover the operating expenses of teaching programs. In the past, except for the rather small subsidies to the land grant colleges, federal programs in higher education have involved either payments made directly to students, or payments made to institutions for buildings or research, but not for the operating expenses associated with teaching activities. The NIH has made a significant departure from this tradition. Its training grants have as an explicit objective the support of teaching programs in the health sciences, as well as the students who benefit from them. (The other significant break in the tradition, of course, is the National Defense fellowships, whose accompanying cost-of-education grants also provide direct support for teaching programs, though in a slightly less obvious way.)

The rapid recent growth in the amount of federal money going into the fellowship and training programs of the National Institutes of Health may be seen in Table XII.

Two other bureaus of the Public Health Service operate training programs, although on a much smaller scale than the NIH. The Bureau of Medical Services administers a traineeship program in administration, supervision, and teaching for professional nurses.

The Bureau of State Services makes training grants to schools of public health and offers some direct traineeships to public health students.

TABLE XII. *National Institutes of Health Fellowship and Training Programs, Fiscal Years 1958-60*

(In thousands)

Program	1958	1959	1960
Fellowships	$ 6,431	$10,174	$14,841
Direct traineeships	2,092	2,503	3,052
Training grants	31,940	49,204	73,744
Total	$40,463	$61,882	$91,637

SOURCE: U. S. Public Health Service, *Grants and Awards by the National Institutes of Health*, 1958 Supplement, p. 2; 1959, Part II, p. 1; 1960, Part II, p. 1.

Atomic Energy Commission Fellowships

In an effort to relieve the postwar shortage of scientists, by helping able students to get advanced training in the sciences, the Atomic Energy Commission early in its history established a group of graduate fellowships in the physical, biological, and medical sciences. Both predoctoral and postdoctoral fellowships were offered in the physical and biological sciences, as well as a small number of postdoctoral awards in medical research. The fellowships carried stipends sufficient to allow the recipients to spend full time on their studies, and fellows, chosen solely on the basis of ability, were allowed to choose the institutions at which they wished to enroll. Within the general areas of physical, biological, and medical science, no attempt was made to attract students to particular specialized fields. The whole idea was to allow highly qualified young scientists to pursue their own interests, not to train particular types of scientific specialists.

The program started in 1948-49 with the award of about 200 fellowships. In each of the following three years, roughly 300 new fellowships were awarded and some existing ones were renewed. Then the program was terminated and no new awards were made after 1951-52, although the AEC continued to consider renewal applications from fellows who had not yet completed their studies. By this time, the National Science Foundation had come into existence, and the decision was made that NSF was a more appropriate agency to handle a fellowship program of this type. Part of the reason for this decision was that Congress had made the administration of the AEC program both complicated and expensive by attaching a rider to the AEC appropriations act in 1950 stipulating that all AEC fellows must have full security clearance. Only a small minority of AEC fellows were actually working on classified projects, and these, of course, had always had to have security clearance. The necessity of going through the whole clearance procedure for the other fellows added considerably to the expense of the program.

Although the Atomic Energy Commission relinquished its general fellowship program, it retained and has expanded several more specialized programs designed to train scientists in particular fields closely related to atomic energy. These fields include reactor technology, health physics, radiation control, and the special industrial medicine and hygiene problems of the atomic energy industry. The AEC has arranged for particular universities to offer instruction to graduate students in these fields, often in conjunction with on-the-job training at an AEC installation. Stipends of various sizes and allowances for dependents are provided, and AEC pays tuition or its equivalent to the universities. The largest program involves 150 special fellowships in nuclear science and engineering—mainly reactor technology—offered at 48 participating institutions. Seventy-five fellowships are offered at six institutions for a year of graduate study in health physics, combined with 10 weeks of special training at an AEC installation.

National Science Foundation Fellowships

The act of Congress establishing the National Science Foundation in 1950 specifically directed the NSF to support scientific education by awarding graduate fellowships in the mathematical, physical, medical, biological, engineering, and other sciences. The program started in fiscal year 1952 with a comparatively modest budget of $1.5 million—a budget which had expanded to $13.5 million by fiscal 1961, as the fellowships were increased both in number and in variety. In 1952, 537 graduate students and 38 postdoctoral scientists were awarded NSF fellowships; by 1960, NSF was awarding 4,000 fellowships under nine seperate programs.

TABLE XIII. *National Science Foundation Fellowships Awarded in Fiscal Year 1960 for Fiscal 1961*

Program	Awards
Postdoctoral	180
Senior postdoctoral	75
Secondary school teachers (summer)	500
Science faculty	285
North Atlantic Treaty Organization	41
Organization for European Economic Cooperation	27
"Regular" graduate	1,200
Cooperative graduate	1,190
Teaching assistants (summer)	580
Total	4,078

SOURCE: U. S. National Science Foundation Press Releases.

Each of the nine programs has a somewhat different objective. The postdoctoral fellowships for advanced study or research are for scientists who have recently completed graduate work, and the "senior" postdoctoral fellowships are for those who have had doctorates for five years or more. The NSF fellowships for science teachers are supposed to give them a respite from instructional duties in which to improve their capacity for stimulating teaching by engaging in further study and research. There are fellowships for college faculty as well as summer fellowships for secondary school teachers of science. The NSF also administers two programs, paid out of the State Department budget, which enable American scientists to do advanced work in European institutions. These are the North Atlantic Treaty Organization postdoctoral fellowships and the Organization for European Economic Cooperation senior visiting fellowships in science. Both the "regular" graduate fellowships and the cooperative graduate fellowships support predoctoral students in the sciences, and the summer fellowships for teaching assistants are designed to make the holding of teaching assistantships more attractive to graduate students.

All NSF fellowships carry stipends large enough to cover essential living expenses in an academic community and allow the holder to devote full time to his studies for the duration of the fellowship. The "regular" graduate fellowships, for example, pay $1,800 to first-year students, $2,000 in subsequent years, and $2,200 in the terminal year—plus modest allowances for dependents and necessary travel. The cooperative graduate fellowships pay $2,200 (without allowances) to which the institution may, if it so desires, add as much as $800. Under the graduate program, NSF pays tuition and all necessary fees incurred by the fellows. Under the cooperative graduate program the institutions receive standard cost-of-education payments ($1,800 per fellow) in lieu of tuition and fees. Teaching assistants on summer fellowships get $50 to $75 a week for the summer session, plus tuition and fees.

The system for awarding NSF fellowships for graduate students warrants rather detailed discussion, because it illustrates some of the problems involved in setting up a graduate fellowship program on the national level—especially the problem of what, if anything, to do about geographical distribution.

The National Science Foundation Act specifies that fellowships shall be awarded "solely on the basis of ability," except that, where several candidates are considered by NSF to be of "substantially equal ability" and they cannot all be awarded fellowships, the available fellowships shall be "awarded to the applicants in such a manner as will tend to result in a wide distribution of . . . fellowships among the States, Territories, possessions and the District of Columbia."

Under the "regular" graduate fellowship program, which began in 1952, fellowships are awarded to candidates selected by NSF aided by its advisory committees. Applicants are required to take an examination measuring their scientific aptitude and achievement. The scores on these examinations, plus academic records, and recommendations from persons familiar with the candidate's work are sent directly to NSF, and are then evaluated by panels of scientists reporting to NSF. The panels of scientists are requested to put the "outstanding" applications (approximately the top 5 per cent) into a separate file and to arrange the remaining applications in groups of "substantially equal ability." All of the outstanding group are offered fellowships. If there are not enough funds available for all of the next highest group, then the home states of the applicants become important. The remaining fellowships are allocated among the states in such a way that the total number of fellowships received by applicants from a given state are approximately proportional to the number of students from that state enrolled in college anywhere in the United States. Then the fellowships allocated to a particular state are awarded to individual applicants on the basis of still another formula. This is designed to make the total number of awards in a given field of study and at a given level of graduate work (first year, second year, and so forth) approximately proportional to the number of applicants in that field and level.

Two aspects of this seemingly complicated procedure are especially interesting. One is that NSF makes no attempt to establish quotas for various types of scientists based on anticipated labor force needs. If twice as many botanists as physicists apply for fellowships then, other things being equal, twice as many botanists as physicists will get fellowships. It makes no difference if botanists are expected to be less scarce than physicists in the future. Second, the geographical distribution is based on the applicant's home state, but, once he receives a fellowship, he can use it at any "appropriate" American or foreign institution which will accept him— and NSF fellows generally have little trouble getting accepted.

This freedom to choose any institution led to very great concentration of NSF graduate fellows in a few well-known institutions. Over half of the 1,200 students awarded fellowships in 1960, as shown in Table XIV, chose six institutions in only three states, while 14 other institutions accounted for a majority of the rest.

The tendency of its graduate fellows to flock to a relatively small number of places has laid NSF open to considerable criticism. No one has disputed that excellent scientific training, possibly the best in the world, was available at Harvard, MIT, and other "big name" schools which are getting most of the NSF fellows. Many observers have questioned, however, whether the over-all objective of strengthening graduate education in the sciences is best served by this type of fellowship program.

TABLE XIV. *National Science Foundation "Regular" Graduate Fellowships, Fiscal Year 1960*

Institution	Number		Per Cent of Total	
Harvard (including Radcliffe)	182			
Massachusetts Institute of Technology	114			
University of California (Berkeley)	106	652	54	
California Institute of Technology	103			
Princeton	87			
Stanford	60			
Next 14 institutions		333	28	
Remaining 77 institutions		215	18	
Total (97 institutions)		1,200	100	

It has been alleged that the NSF program was tending to over-crowd the universities which already had exceptionally strong science departments and was actually making it more difficult for less famous institutions which were building up good science departments to attract capable graduate students. If the students of very high ability, it was argued, had not obtained NSF fellowships they would have accepted other fellowships or assistantships at one of the fairly wide range of these good, not so famous but less crowded, institutions. One might expect, of course, that, since fellowships are usually awarded to the best students, a major increase in the total amount of fellowship aid available at all institutions would tend to lower the average ability of fellows generally. It was alleged by some, however, that the NSF program was substantially lowering the average ability of fellowship holders in many places, while raising it at a few.

Actually, even the institutions attracting substantial numbers of NSF fellows were not entirely happy with the program. The NSF fellows were appointed by Washington, received their stipends from Washington, addressed their complaints to Washington, and often seemed to regard themselves as visitors on the campus rather than regular students of the institutions they were attending. Some felt that NSF fellows would be better integrated into the academic community if the institutions were given a greater role in selecting the candidates and administering the program.

To meet these objections, in 1959, NSF established a new program of fellowships known as the cooperative graduate fellowships. However, it retained the "regular" graduate fellowships. The cooperative program is approximately the same size as the "regular" graduate fellowship program, but it is designed to distribute NSF fellowships more widely among institutions, and to give the universities themselves a greater part in selecting the fellows.

It was not an easy matter to devise a selection procedure which would accomplish these objectives without violating the statutory provision that all NSF fellowships must be awarded solely on the basis of ability. Under the procedure adopted, an applicant for a cooperative fellowship applies, not to NSF, but directly to the institution he wishes to attend, furnishing substantially the same test scores and information about himself that he would have submitted to NSF in applying for a regular graduate fellowship. (He may not apply for both.) The faculty and administration of the institution evaluate the applications, rank them in what they consider their order of merit and forward them to NSF.[11] Then, NSF turns the applications over to its panels of scientists with instructions to treat them the same as the applications for "regular" graduate fellowships; that is, to put them into quality groups without regard

[11] Each institution is assigned a maximum number of applicants which it can recommend, based on the graduate degrees in science it has produced in the recent past, but these recommendation quotas are not of great importance, since the institution must forward all eligible applications, recommended or not, to the NSF.

to the ranking made by the institutions. Fellowships are first awarded to the students in the top or "outstanding" group. Then, if there are not enough fellowships for all the students in the next group "of substantially equal ability," the available fellowships are allocated to the participating schools in such a way as to make the total number of fellows at each institution roughly proportional to its recent production of graduate degrees in science. The institutions' own rankings are respected in awarding fellowships to particular individuals in this second group. In effect, this procedure is a compromise between that used in awarding "regular" NSF graduate fellowships, under which no attempt is made to insure a dispersion among institutions, and that used in the awarding of National Defense fellowships, under which all the emphasis is on distributing fellowships among institutions and no attempt is made to ensure that the fellows at different places are of equal ability.

The cooperative fellowship program has, in fact, resulted in a greater dispersion of NSF fellows. The top six institutions shown in Table XIV, which attracted over half the recipients of "regular" graduate fellowships in 1960, received only 14 per cent of the cooperative fellowship recipients for that year. The rest were fairly widely distributed among 127 other institutions.

The growing number of opportunities for predoctoral students in the sciences to obtain fellowships or serve as research assistants led to a problem which inspired creation of the NSF summer fellowships for teaching assistants. Many institutions had been complaining that they were having difficulty inducing qualified graduate students to assist with undergraduate teaching in the sciences. This was because the best students either accepted fellowships, which entailed no obligations except progress toward a degree, or research assistantships, under which they were frequently well paid for doing research that could be used as the basis for a dissertation. Teaching assistants usually received less money and had to spend a great many hours a week preparing for classes, meeting with students, and grading papers—all of which was undoubtedly good experience, but did not help them meet the course and research requirements of the doctorate. The NSF summer fellowships attract teaching assistants by giving them a subsidized respite from teaching duties during which the graduate student can devote himself exclusively to study and research. As in the cooperative fellowship program, students submit applications for the summer fellowships directly to their own institutions and selections are made by NSF on the basis of ability and institutional recommendations.

SELECTED REFERENCES FOR CHAPTER 4

1) U. S. Veterans Administration, *Annual Reports.*
2) Bradford Morse, "The Veteran and his Education," *Higher Education,* March 1960.
3) U. S. President's Commission on Veterans' Benefits, *Readjustment Benefits: Education and Training, and Employment and Unemployment,* Vol. III, Staff Report No. 9, Part B, 1956.
4) U. S. President's Commission on Higher Education, *Higher Education for American Democracy* (six volumes), 1947.
5) U. S. President's Committee on Education Beyond the High School, *Second Report to the President,* July 1957.
6) U. S. Senate, Committee on Labor and Public Welfare, *Science and Education for National Defense,* 1958.
7) U. S. Office of Education, *The National Defense Student Loan Program, A Two-Year Report* (OE 55019), 1961.
8) ———, *Report on The National Defense Education Act Fiscal Year Ending June 30, 1960* (OE 10004-60), 1961.

5

Federal Funds for
Campus Buildings

FEDERAL AID FOR CONSTRUCTION of college and university buildings is another relatively recent activity, dating back only about 30 years. During the Depression of the 1930's, to provide employment, the federal government helped many public institutions of higher education build dormitories and academic facilities. After World War II, the government turned over large amounts of surplus federal property to both public and private institutions to help them provide space for the "GI bulge" in enrollment. Beginning in 1950, Congress authorized the government to make loans for college and university housing. The college housing loan program, which benefits both public and private institutions, has become a major source of funds for dormitories and similar facilities.

The Depression Programs and
Postwar Surplus Properties

A visitor to almost any tax-supported university is likely to find, if he is a reader of ivy-covered cornerstones and bronze plaques in entrance halls, that many campus buildings date from the 1930's and were constructed in part with federal funds administered by the Public Works Administration (PWA) or, in some cases, by the Works Progress Administration (WPA). This federal building program was designed primarily to put men to work, not to aid higher education, but it contributed substantially to the expansion and modernization of plant in public colleges and universities.

The PWA was authorized to make grants to states, municipalities, and other public bodies to help finance various types of construction, including school and college buildings. Under the original act, passed in 1933, the federal contribution to an individual project could not exceed 30 per cent of the cost of labor and materials. Further legislation, in 1935, authorized the PWA to make grants covering as much as 45 per cent of the total cost of a project. The remaining 55 per cent had to be supplied by the state or local sponsor of the project, but part of this amount could be financed by the sale of bonds to the PWA.

TABLE XV. *PWA College Building Projects, March 1, 1939*

Number of Projects	662
Funds supplied by applicant	$ 87,258,807
PWA allotment	110,905,882
Loans	(30,458,829)
Grants	(80,447,053)
Total cost	$198,164,689

SOURCE: *America Builds: The Record of the PWA,* p. 288, as cited in "Selected References to Chapter 5."

Most state universities, and all but eight of the land grant colleges, undertook PWA construction. The University of Alabama, for example, had 13 separate projects including a science building and several dormitories. These cost about $2,567,000, of which a PWA grant supplied $1,153,000. The University of Washington built a library wing, several dormitories, an infirmary, additions to its power plant, a chemistry building, and an aerodynamics laboratory at a total cost of about $2,848,000. Of this amount, PWA grants supplied about $1,000,000, and an additional $435,000 came from PWA loans. The Universities of Indiana, Illinois, Arkansas, Kansas, Maryland, and Louisville had PWA help in expanding their medical schools. In all, 662 college building projects had been started by PWA, at a cost of almost $200 million, by March of 1939, when the program was approaching termination.

Since the Depression building program was conceived as a public works program, private institutions were not eligible for PWA grants. The distinction between public and private, however, is occasionally blurred by the existence of institutions which the courts have ruled are public for some purposes and private for others. In at least one such borderline case, Syracuse University, an institution which is usually considered private received a PWA loan to build its medical school.[1]

The Public Works Administration was not the only recovery agency which aided campus construction. A number of tax-supported institutions also utilized Works Progress Administration labor on building and modernization projects. In general, the WPA supplied the workers, and the institution was expected to finance materials and other costs from its own funds.

At the end of World War II, the federal government gave away—or sold at nominal prices—large amounts of surplus property to nonprofit educational institutions of various types, both public and private. Sometimes, whole Army camps were turned over to universities. More frequently, surplus property was moved from camps to campuses, often at government expense. Between 1945 and 1948, the Public Housing Administration alone spent $160 million dismantling, transporting, and reconstructing surplus residential buildings for college use. Prefabricated barracks, quonset huts, officers clubs, and the like were moved from military bases to colleges and universities—sometimes to rehouse GI's who had recently vacated them. Some of this "temporary" housing is still in use.

The College Housing Loan Program

The disposal of surplus federal property to the colleges was followed by a more permanent program of federal loans for the construction of residential facilities at higher educational institutions.

[1] The medical center at Syracuse in 1950 became part of the State University of New York.

The Housing Act of 1950 authorized the federal government to make long-term loans to colleges and universities for the construction of faculty and student housing, including dormitories, apartments, single-family units, and improvements to existing residential buildings. All nonprofit institutions of higher education, both private and public, were declared eligible to apply for the loans. The loans have not been extended to theological schools, but other church-related colleges have participated in the program. Additional legislation, in 1957, made teaching hospitals eligible to apply for loans to finance the construction of housing for interns and student nurses.

The program got off to a slow start. The original legislation authorized the Housing and Home Finance Agency to lend up to $300 million, but while the Korean War was in progress the President released only part of this amount. Also, he required that all loans be defense-related; all had to go to colleges which had special housing needs arising from the expansion of ROTC units, defense research contracts, and the like. Despite the removal of this restriction in August 1953, by the end of 1955 approved loans still totaled less than $200 million.

The program expanded rapidly as a result of amendments to the Housing Act passed in 1955. The authorization was increased to $500 million, and the definition of eligible projects was expanded to include cafeterias, dining halls, student unions, infirmaries, and other service facilities, as well as actual housing. Perhaps more important was a lowering of the interest rate which applied to the loans.

From 1953 to 1955, the interest rate charged the colleges was based on the market yields of long-term Treasury bonds (bonds with maturities of 10 years or more). The 1955 amendments set the interest rate at either 2¾ per cent or the average interest rate on all Treasury interest-bearing obligations at the end of the last fiscal year plus ¼ per cent—whichever was higher. This change in the law brought about a reduction in the rate on college housing loans from 3¼ per cent in fiscal 1955 to 2¾ per cent for fiscal year 1956. The lower rate made it advantageous for public institutions to borrow from the federal government rather than in the state and municipal bond market. It thus resulted in a considerable increase in

TABLE XVI. *College Housing Loans Approved, by Type of Institution*

(Dollars in thousands)

Calendar Year	Private Institutions		Public Institutions		Total	
	Number	Amount [a]	Number	Amount [a]	Number	Amount [a]
1951	10	$ 9,806	7	$ 7,089	17	$ 16,895
1952	16	13,193	11	11,220	27	24,413
1953	43	34,064	20	17,481	63	51,545
1954	53	30,406	15	17,951	68	48,357
1955	53	30,528	14	16,625	67	47,153
1956	116	90,019	75	101,212	191	191,231
1957	122	98,715	80	114,696	202	213,411
1958	120	95,037	88	139,485	208	234,522
1959	102	72,600	54	63,393	156	135,993
1960	104	93,004	81	100,037	185	193,041
1961 (half)	134	132,601	65	100,016	199	232,617
Less rescissions [b] .	23	15,475	23	28,109	46	43,584
Total net approvals	716	$551,897	422	$561,080	1,138	$1,112,977 [c]

SOURCE: U. S. Housing and Home Finance Agency, *Thirteenth Annual Report, 1959*, p. 256. 1960 and 1961 figures supplied by HHFA. Hospitals are excluded.

a Original amount of approved loan, subject to adjustment for changes in project cost.

b Withdrawals after loan approval, primarily because of financing from non-government sources.

c After adjustments for changes in project cost, this net total stood at $1,363,183,000 on June 30, 1961.

applications, especially from public colleges and universities. Since then, the interest rate has risen somewhat—it was 3½ per cent in fiscal 1961, and has been set at 3⅝ per cent for fiscal 1962. However, since interest rates in the private sector have also risen, borrowing from the government for college housing continues to be advantageous to both public and private institutions.

Congress increased the amount authorized for college housing loans to $750 million in 1956; $925 million in 1957; $1,175 million in 1959; and $1,675 million in 1960. The Housing Act of 1961 authorized further increases of $300 million a year for four years, which will bring the College Housing Loan Revolving Fund to $2,875 million by July 1, 1964. Table XVI shows loans to public and private institutions approved by the end of June 1961.

Of all eligible institutions, close to half had applied for loans by the end of fiscal year 1959. Two-thirds of all state institutions and over half of all eligible private colleges had filed applications. As may be seen in Table XVII, municipal institutions and private junior colleges—many of which do not provide housing or dining facilities for students—have not participated in the program to the same extent as others.

TABLE XVII. *Institutions of Higher Education Which Had Applied for College Housing Loans, June 30, 1959*

Type	Number	Per Cent
State institutions ᵃ	345	66
Municipal institutions	288	14
Private junior colleges	199	24
Other private institutions	890	54
Total eligible institutions	1,743	45

SOURCE: U. S. Housing and Home Finance Agency, Community Facilities Administration.

ᵃ Excluding 21 institutions served by the New York State Dormitory Authority.

In order to get a loan, a college must demonstrate a need for additional faculty or student housing or for related facilities. Present need is taken more seriously than anticipated future need, and a college is generally required to show that its current student body or faculty is inadequately housed. Sometimes, however, when it seems virtually certain that an increase in enrollment will occur if housing is available, loans are made.

When the government approves a project, it reserves the necessary funds and agrees to purchase the bonds of the institutions if, after adequate advertisement, no private investors can be found who will purchase the bonds on equally favorable terms. The bonds issued by state and municipal institutions often attract private investors because the interest on such bonds is exempt from federal income taxation. But private investors are rarely willing to take the bonds of private institutions on terms as favorable as those offered by the government.

The borrowing college or university must pledge revenues, either from the project itself or from other sources, which are deemed sufficient to pay off its debt. The government is extremely careful to protect itself against default by the institutions, for it was not the intent of the program to subsidize higher education by "forgiving" any of these loans. As of the end of June 1961, after operation of the program for a decade, no college had yet defaulted on any interest or principal due.

Are College Housing Loans a Subsidy?

Whether or not one regards the college housing loan program as a government subsidy to higher education depends on how one defines a "subsidy." It is possible to argue that a subsidy arises when the government transfers resources to someone else at a price which is not sufficient to cover the cost of these resources to the government. Here, the difference between the price charged the user and the cost to the government would be the amount of the subsidy. By this definition, educational institutions are not being subsidized under the college housing loan program as long as the interest rate they have to pay is sufficient to cover the cost of the money to the government plus the administrative expense of the program.

The problem is: What is the cost of this money to the government? Is it the interest rate the Treasury is currently paying on all its outstanding obligations? Or is it the rate the Treasury would have to pay to borrow new funds now? Is it the average rate the Treasury is paying (or would have to pay) on obligations of all maturities or only on obligations of maturities comparable to the college housing loans? Discussion of these issues can become extremely technical.[2] As noted above, under the law as now written, the colleges are charged a rate of interest equal to the average interest rate on all Treasury obligations outstanding at the end of the previous fiscal year (plus ¼ per cent to cover the risks and expenses of the program). This means that, when interest rates are rising, the government is likely to be lending to the colleges at a lower rate than that at which the Treasury can currently borrow.

Alternatively, one can take the position that a subsidy arises whenever government intervention enables someone to obtain resources at a price lower than he would have paid without the intervention. From this point of view, the amount of the subsidy would be the difference between the price paid and the ordinary market price in the absence of government action.[3] In this sense, the college housing loan program does involve a subsidy. By lending money for campus housing at less than the market rate of interest, the federal government is channeling some of the nation's resources into college housing which would go elsewhere if institutions of higher education had to rely on private sources and on state and local governments to finance this type of building. This reallocation of resources toward college housing is precisely the objective of the program.

Academic Facilities

There has been considerable support in Congress for extending the coverage of the college housing loan program to include instructional buildings as well as college housing. A provision to this

[2] For a clear exposition of these and related points see Arnold H. Diamond, "Interest Rates for Government Lending Programs," *National Tax Journal,* December 1960, pp. 320-28.

[3] See Robert I. Hubbell, "Concealed Subsidies in the Federal Budget," *National Tax Journal,* September 1957, pp. 214-27.

effect was incorporated in a housing bill which passed the Senate in 1958 and then died in the House. Loans for classroom buildings and other instructional facilities were also included in the provisions of the omnibus housing bill which Congress passed in 1959, and President Eisenhower vetoed.

The Eisenhower Administration not only opposed loans for instructional facilities but also opposed federal lending for college housing. It proposed an alternative under which the government would have guaranteed payments of interest and principal on bonds sold by institutions of higher education to private investors for the purpose of financing housing or instructional buildings. The Eisenhower Administration's bill (S. 1017, 86th Congress) also would have authorized the federal government to pay 25 per cent of the principal of such loans in equal installments over 20 years. This "debt retirement assistance" was supposed to compensate the colleges for the higher interest rates they would have to pay private lenders.[4] The bill did not receive enough support on Capitol Hill to reach a floor vote.

The Kennedy Administration favors federal loans for instructional buildings, but would separate this program from the college housing loan program. The Administration-sponsored bill (H.R. 5266, 87th Congress) proposed that up to $300 million a year for five years ($1.5 billion in all) be made available for loans to public and private nonprofit institutions of higher education for the construction of academic facilities—including classrooms, laboratories, libraries, and administrative and service buildings. The loans would be for periods up to 50 years with interest at the same rate as the college housing loans. The colleges would finance one-quarter of the cost of each project themselves, and no more than 12.5 per cent of the money would be loaned to institutions in any one state. The academic facilities program would be administered by the Office of Education, not the Housing and Home Finance Agency.

The House Committee on Education and Labor, however, rejected the Administration bill and on May 26, 1961, reported favor-

[4] The federal guarantees would have applied only to private nonprofit institutions, not to state and municipal institutions whose securities are exempt from federal income tax. The "debt retirement assistance" would have applied to both public and private nonprofit institutions.

ably on a substitute bill (H.R. 7215) with somewhat different provisions. The House Committee bill would authorize $120 million a year for five years for loans, plus $180 million annually for outright grants to colleges and universities for academic facilities. The grant funds would be allotted to the states on the basis of college and high school enrollment, and could not be used to finance more than one-third of the cost of any single building project. The Senate Committee on Education and Labor reported a bill authorizing loans for college and university construction and matching grants for junior colleges. At the time this was written, Congress had not taken further action on either bill.

SELECTED REFERENCES FOR CHAPTER 5

1) U. S. Public Works Administration, *America Builds, The Record of the PWA,* 1939.
2) Arnold H. Diamond, "The College Housing Program: Its History and Operations," *The Educational Record,* July 1957, pp. 1-16.
3) U. S. Housing and Home Finance Agency, *Annual Reports.*

6

The Limited Role of Federal Educational Institutions

IN GENERAL, the federal government has aided, and cooperated with, private, state, and local colleges in preference to establishing higher educational institutions of its own. The military academies are major exceptions, but the government has not expected the academies to carry the full burden of military higher education. It has relied heavily on civilian institutions as well. There has not always been unanimous agreement, however, that federal institutions of higher education should play such a limited role. Proposals for a national university have a long history, and support for other types of federal institutions of higher education has cropped up from time to time, both in and out of Congress.

The Military Academies

Educating the professional soldier has long been regarded as a responsibility of the federal government, although it has not always been clear that this responsibility involved higher education. When the United States Military Academy at West Point was founded in 1802, it bore little resemblance to an academic institution. The cadets were essentially apprentice officers and received no formal classroom instruction. Eventually, classes in military tactics and engineering were organized and classroom buildings were built.

By the mid-nineteenth century, West Point had become a well-recognized engineering school, and one of the country's main sources of trained engineers for both civilian and military employment. Entrance requirements were low, however, and instruction in areas other than engineering and tactics was largely neglected. Only gradually was the curriculum broadened and the level of instruction raised until collegiate-level courses were being offered, not only in military and engineering subjects, but also in other academic disciplines.

This process was a slow one, and it was not until after World War I that the Academy gained recognition as a full-fledged institution of higher education. In 1933, Congress authorized West Point to grant the Bachelor of Science degree. The slowness of this evolution was at least partly a result of congressional feeling that it was not the job of the federal government to run a college, and also that allowing the Academy to raise its entrance requirements would tend to limit careers as Army officers to the sons of the wealthy in a day when public secondary education was not generally available.

The history of the Naval Academy at Annapolis is similar. It was founded in 1845, but only slowly, and over some congressional opposition, did it become a collegiate-level institution. Coast Guard and Merchant Marine Academies were founded later, and the newest addition, the Air Force Academy in Colorado, opened in 1955. All of the military academies are now accredited colleges offering bachelors degrees, and are preparing their students to become career officers in the various services. Admission is by congressional appointment after a competitive examination, and no tuition is charged. The government bears the full cost of the students' education, including room and board and allowances for travel and expenses.

Evolution of the Reserve Officer Training Corps

Federal concern with the education of the nonprofessional soldier is of more recent origin, although the concept of calling on a citizen militia in a national emergency goes back to the Minutemen.

In 1819, Captain Alden Partridge founded a private military academy at Norwich, Vermont, with the objective of training civilians to serve as militia officers; and several private military academies grew up in the South in the pre-Civil War period. During the Civil War, the Union found itself desperately short of trained officers, and in 1862, when Congress passed the Morrill Act establishing the land grant colleges, it specifically directed them to teach "military tactics." Morrill, incidentally, was a friend of Partridge, and familiar with the instruction offered at Norwich.

The statute said only that military tactics should be included in the curriculum, and for a while the land grant colleges had almost no guidance from the War Department on what to teach. Most of them simply instituted marching drill, sometimes compulsory and sometimes not, under the supervision of some faculty member who happened to be a former Army officer. In 1866, Congress authorized the War Department to issue small arms and artillery to the students and to detail regular officers to the colleges to serve as instructors. But the Department showed only sporadic interest in the college programs until the outbreak of the first World War, frequently alleging that it was unable to spare the necessary officers and equipment. Nevertheless, by 1898, 42 land grant colleges had organized formal military departments, and a few other colleges also had set up programs—on their own initiative but with the approval of the War Department. By 1914, 30,000 college students were taking military instruction, and the land grant colleges were pointing out that more Army officers were graduates of their institutions than of West Point.

The idea of supplementing the peacetime professional Army with a permanent corps of trained reservists evolved just before World War I. Up to this point, some qualified graduates of the college military programs who wanted to serve in the Army had been given regular commissions along with West Point men, but no such thing as a reserve commission existed. The National Defense Act of 1916 created a permanent reserve whose officers were to come from a Reserve Officer Training Corps with units in civilian colleges. The existing college military programs were absorbed into the ROTC system.

The United States entered World War I before the ROTC began to function. The War saw the creation of a Student Army Training Corps into which young men were inducted and then reassigned to colleges for special training. Student Army Training Corps units were established at a large number of colleges in the academic year 1917-18, but the War was over before the program got into full operation.

After the War, ROTC units were re-established in the land grant colleges and in a number of other institutions, including some private ones.[1] Regular army officers were assigned to these units as instructors, and the programs offered were standardized and made somewhat more rigorous. They consisted of two years of basic training which was compulsory in the land grant colleges and in some others. Selected volunteers then received two more years of advanced training leading to a reserve commission. Although the Army strongly encouraged the compulsory feature, it did not absolutely insist upon it. In 1923, pacifist sentiment in the state legislature forced the University of Wisconsin to make ROTC participation voluntary for a few years. The Army accepted the situation, as it did in Minnesota after 1933.

In 1942, ROTC was suspended as too slow a method of training officers in wartime. However, large numbers of men were drafted into the services and put into special training programs which utilized college facilities and faculty members. Again, after the War, the ROTC was reactivated on essentially the prewar basis. By this time, the Air Force had developed a separate but similar program of its own.

The Navy, which had ROTC units in only a few colleges before World War II (eight units in 1938), introduced an innovation in 1946 known as the Holloway Plan. In an effort to induce more young men of high ability to become naval officers, the Navy offered to pay all the expenses through four years of college of a selected group of officer candidates who would agree to accept commissions on graduation and serve a specified number of years on active duty.

---

[1] The Negro land grant colleges, however, were largely ignored by the Army until after World War II. Edward D. Eddy, Jr., *Colleges for our Land and Time: The Land-Grant Idea in American Education,* Harper, 1956, p. 262.

About 7,000 college students a year are now being subsidized under the Holloway Plan. In addition, a somewhat larger number of students are enrolled in the ordinary Naval ROTC units.

The Holloway Plan may presage a shift of emphasis in the ROTC programs of all the services. With warfare becoming increasingly technical, the idea of calling on the partially trained reserve officer to lead citizen soldiers in a national emergency seems less and less realistic. The cost of training an officer to be useful in a modern war is increasing rapidly. It costs many thousands of dollars to train a jet pilot, for example, and this investment does not pay off if the pilot returns to civilian life after two or three years. On the other hand, pilots are most useful when they are young and not all of them can expect to become generals, since not that many generals are needed. This means that the services need to recruit officers who will serve on extended active duty (five to 10 years or more), but not necessarily expect to find a lifetime career in the service. The Navy is now looking increasingly to its ROTC programs (especially the Holloway Plan) as a means of recruiting able officers for extended active duty, and the Air Force has altered its advanced ROTC program with this in mind.

The question of compulsory versus voluntary ROTC training continues to be unresolved. If the main purpose of ROTC is to attract relatively small numbers of college graduates to military careers, rather than to expose larger numbers to a smattering of military rudiments, then presumably compulsory ROTC should be abandoned. Instead, more selective and more attractive programs for volunteers should be set up. The Army and the Air Force, however, are ambivalent about abandoning the compulsory feature. The Army, which still recognizes the need for a reserve of citizen soldiers as well as for career and extended active duty officers, has continued to encourage the institutions to keep the first two years compulsory, although the encouragement has recently been less vociferous than in the past. The Air Force looks on its program of basic training for all freshmen and sophomores in certain institutions as a contribution to "air-age citizenship." In 1959, the three services had ROTC units in 313 colleges and universities; in 177 of these, ROTC was compulsory.

The financial arrangements between the services and the colleges with ROTC units have been quite simple—no money changes hands. The government supplies instructors, uniforms, books, and equipment. The institution supplies classrooms, drill grounds, and other facilities and absorbs the overhead costs.

For a long time, the institutions have been trying to get the government to take over a larger share of the total costs, especially the construction and maintenance of permanent facilities. The colleges argue that it is the job of the military services to provide for national defense and to train military officers. Therefore, there is no justification for exploiting the limited resources of educational institutions by using their facilities for this purpose without compensation. The services have replied, however, that it is the traditional function of universities to prepare students for careers, especially for careers of public importance, such as medicine, science, and government service—both civilian and military. The government is willing to pay most of the cost of ROTC, but there is no reason why the universities should not contribute their share.

From a more practical point of view, the Defense Department has been unwilling to invest in permanent construction on college campuses since these "sunk" costs would make it much more difficult to disband particular ROTC units on short notice. Actually, although the colleges have often complained about the high cost of maintaining ROTC units, they have usually been reluctant to have their units disbanded. At the end of the Korean War, the Army and Air Force wanted to eliminate some of their smaller ROTC units, but changed their minds in the face of resistance from the colleges concerned. Apparently, the colleges felt that if they did not have ROTC units they would be more likely to suffer a severe drop in enrollment in the event of a national emergency. The Navy, in 1958, proposed the reduction of the cost of the Holloway Plan by increasing the proportion of subsidized students in relatively low-tuition institutions. This drew cries of protest from the higher-tuition private institutions whose quotas were being reduced.

The Defense Department is still unwilling to construct permanent facilities for ROTC use. But, in the face of mounting insistence from the colleges, it has stated that it favors legislation which would enable the government to compensate the colleges for the current expenses of carrying ROTC programs. Under the Department proposal, a college with an ROTC unit would receive a flat sum per graduate commissioned—this sum to "approximate the average all institutions must furnish out of pocket to support one ROTC student for four years." [2] This proposal would be of considerable help to the colleges. However, it would be of greatest help to the institutions in which ROTC was not compulsory, since they tend to have much higher ratios of commissioned graduates to total ROTC enrollment. Hence, it would increase the incentive for colleges to make their ROTC programs voluntary.

In addition to regular and reserve officer training, the military services use civilian institutions for certain types of in-service training of military personnel. For example, they frequently send career officers for a year or more of graduate training at civilian universities, paying their tuition and expenses as well as their regular salaries for this period.

Gallaudet College and Howard University

Two institutions of higher education in the District of Columbia receive special federal support: Gallaudet College and Howard University.

Gallaudet College was established by Act of Congress in 1864 under the name of the National Deaf-Mute College. It provides college instruction for deaf students from all parts of the country and facilities for training teachers to teach in schools for the deaf. A nonprofit corporation, it is under private control, but has received federal support since its foundation. At present, Gallaudet receives about 65 per cent of its current income and virtually all of its building funds from the federal government. [3]

Howard University was founded in 1867 to help fill the urgent

[2] Charles C. Finucane, "The Future of ROTC," *Higher Education*, December 1959, p. 12.

[3] U. S. Department of Health, Education and Welfare, *Handbook on Programs of the Department of Health, Education and Welfare*, 1961 Edition, p. 17.

need for educational facilities for Negroes. It was established as a private nonprofit corporation controlled by a self-perpetuating board of trustees, but it had close contact with the government and received federal support from the beginning. In fact, General Oliver Otis Howard—after whom the University was named and who was active in its foundation—was president of the University during some of the years when, from 1865 to 1874, he was Commissioner of the Freedmen's Bureau. In the light of modern concern over conflicts of interest, this seems a decidedly curious arrangement, since the University was receiving a major part of its support from the Freedmen's Bureau.

Although Howard was called a "university" from the beginning, most of its early students had received little prior schooling. Gradually, it was able to raise the standard and levels of instruction and obtain accreditation for its liberal arts college and professional schools. A large proportion of its graduates have taken teacher training courses and returned to the South to teach in Negro schools. Many others have obtained training in law, medicine, engineering, architecture, and other professional courses, which was usually unavailable to them in the public universities of the South. By supporting Howard, the federal government took over a function normally performed by state governments—that of providing public education at all levels for all residents—but which the Southern states were performing inadequately for their Negro residents.

At present, Howard has an operating budget of about $10 million, a little over half of which is provided by federal appropriations. The federal government also contributes funds for buildings.[4]

Proposals for a National University

The idea of a civilian West Point or a national university has recurred so often in the history of American higher education that it deserves at least brief mention. Although no bill establishing a national university has ever come really close to enactment by Congress, the proposal in various forms has had the support of at least

[4] *Ibid.*, p. 15.

eight presidents and an impressive list of educators and educational organizations.

The Constitutional Convention in 1787 discussed the inclusion of a clause giving Congress the power to establish a national university. The fact that such a clause was not included in the Constitution does not seem to have been primarily caused by any strong opposition to a national university as such. Rather, it seems to have resulted from the view that the clause was unnecessary, since control of the federal district already gave Congress the power to establish a national university in the capital city. The first six presidents—Washington, John Adams, Jefferson, Madison, Monroe, and John Quincy Adams—all favored a national university, although Jefferson seems to have felt that a constitutional amendment would be required. Washington more than once requested Congress to act favorably on the proposal. He had some correspondence with the Commissioners of the District of Columbia about a site for the university, and in his will left to Congress for such an institution shares of stock in the Potomac River Company. This bequest was never accepted by Congress, and it is not known what happened to the shares.

Despite the wishes of the "founding fathers," interest in the proposal seems to have lapsed until after the Civil War. In 1869, John W. Hoyt began a long and ardent campaign for a national university by winning the support of the National Teachers Association (later called the National Education Association) for the measure. A whole series of bills in the 1870's called for the establishment of a national university. Presidents Grant and Hayes called on Congress for favorable action, but still without results. Another flurry of legislative proposals occurred in the late 1890's and another around 1905-07. By that time, the proposal for a national university had the support of the National Association of State Universities as well as the National Education Association, but this backing does not seem to have made any impression on Congress.

The supporters of the national university at the turn of the century seem to have had in mind primarily a graduate institution, supplementing the undergraduate programs of the state universities, most of which then had weak graduate schools, or none at all.

The principal opposition came from the major private institutions of the East, which were striving to develop strong graduate schools. President Eliot of Harvard was particularly vocal in his opposition to the idea, and he was joined by the presidents of Yale and Columbia and also by the supporters of American University in Washington.

In recent years, support for the proposal seems to have died out, although bills calling for the establishment of a national university were introduced as late as the 1930's, and proposals for national institutions of more limited scope have appeared from time to time since World War II. A foreign service academy is suggested periodically. Since the Sputnik scare, there have been several bills introduced to establish a United States Science Academy to do research and graduate-level teaching in the physical and biological sciences. But this idea has not been received with much enthusiasm either on Capitol Hill or in existing universities.

SELECTED REFERENCES FOR CHAPTER 6

1) Gene M. Lyons and John W. Masland, *Education and Military Leadership: A Study of the ROTC*, Princeton University Press, 1959.
2) John W. Masland and Laurence I. Radway, *Soldiers and Scholars, Military Education and National Policy*, Princeton University Press, 1957.
3) Edgar Bruce Wesley, *Proposed: The University of the United States*, University of Minnesota Press, 1936.
4) Carl W. Tvedt, "A Brief History of the National University," *School and Society*, January 10, 1931, pp. 42-47.

7

The Federal Government's Changing Role

THE MOST IMPORTANT FACT about federal policy toward higher education is that there has never been a clearly defined policy. Only rarely has Congress explicitly undertaken the support of higher education. Legislation affecting higher education has been a by-product of some other well-established federal concern, such as agriculture or public health or the disposal of public lands or military needs. This situation seems to be changing; the support of higher education as such is beginning to be recognized as an appropriate federal activity.

The Motivation for Federal Programs

The original land grants to new states for the establishment of state universities were prompted mainly by congressional desire to dispose of public land on favorable terms. Once the precedent had been established, other new states with federal lands within their borders insisted on equivalent grants. The Morrill Act, creating the land grant colleges, was primarily a measure to encourage more scientific agriculture, although it received support from diverse interests—including those eager to establish the principle that all the states were entitled to benefit from the disposition of federal lands.

During the 1930's, the federal financing of buildings at public insti-

118

tutions of higher education was part of a much larger program of public works designed to promote economic recovery by getting men to work, preferably on useful projects. More recently, the principal objective of federal financing of extensive research programs on university campuses and the growing number of fellowships and training grants—most of them in the sciences—has not been to help the colleges and universities involved. Rather, it has been to get the research done in the interests of health and national defense and to train more people to do more research in the future. Even the more general programs of federal help for students under the National Youth Administration and the GI Bill of Rights were not primarily undertaken to strengthen higher education. They were temporary measures to aid recovery from the Depression and readjustment from war, and they were abandoned as soon as these emergencies were over.

The National Defense Education Act may represent the beginning of a new era of explicit recognition of higher education as a legitimate area of federal concern. To be sure, the word "defense" is in the title and there is considerable verbiage about "national security" and the "present emergency." Nevertheless, the Act comes closer to being an out-and-out education measure than any previous legislation. The provision for the student loan program seems to indicate congressional acceptance of the idea that it is in the national interest for the federal government to help undergraduates finance their education on a continuing basis. The action was not taken in order to keep students out of the labor force or to compensate them for military service, but because facilitating their education is desirable. Similarly, the National Defense fellowship program seems to be designed to produce more college teachers in all fields by building up new centers of graduate study in all parts of the country instead of merely producing more defense and health researchers. The efficacy of the measures taken may be questioned, but the intent of the National Defense Education Act clearly was to use federal resources to strengthen higher education generally. This recognition of higher education as a national concern may well turn out to be the most important feature of the Act.

The Stimulation of Higher Education

Although the primary motivation of federal activity has not been educational, federal actions have profoundly affected the development of our system of higher education. If the legislatures of new states had not been prodded into establishing state universities quickly in order to benefit from federal land grants, many of them might have delayed years, even decades. Similarly, if the states had not had the incentive of the Morrill Act to get agricultural and mechanical colleges into operation, many might have neglected this type of education for a long time.

Perhaps more important are the many instances in which the government has used the existing system of higher education to carry out federal programs which might have been undertaken elsewhere. In general, this undoubtedly has strengthened the system. The primary example, of course, is research. In World War I, the government research effort was mainly centered outside universities, but this precedent was not followed in World War II. Instead, existing university laboratories were utilized wherever possible and large new scientific research installations were built on university campuses at federal expense. Some scientists, of course, left the campus for government laboratories and many left smaller colleges for larger institutions but, in general, the government made an effort to use university scientists where they were.

This pattern has continued in the postwar period. It has been especially marked in health as well as in military research. The federal government might have elected to do all or most of the health research in government laboratories, but instead a large part of the program of the National Institutes of Health has been "extramural," designed not only to utilize existing research facilities in hospitals and universities, but to build up these nonfederal facilities for future work.

This tendency to use the existing nonfederal system has not been limited to research. In recent years, the military services have relied more and more on ROTC units to provide officers, even career officers. They might have elected to expand the military academies or found a number of new ones to meet this need. In many instances, the military services and other government agencies have sent career employees to regular colleges and universities for in-service training, rather than attempting to set up training facilities of their own. Suggestions that the federal government establish a "science academy" or a "civil service academy" or even a national university have not been accepted, but very considerable use has been made of existing institutions to train scientists, language experts, public health officers, and other specialists needed for the federal service.

In many other areas, the federal government has been criticized for carrying out programs of its own which failed to utilize existing private or state facilities. In higher education, by contrast, the main criticism leveled at the government has been too much use of the universities for federal purposes. It is alleged that so many federally sponsored activities are being conducted by colleges and universities that their programs are being distorted and their regular teaching functions neglected. There may well be an element of truth in this, but if the federal government had elected to carry out these same programs outside colleges and universities, many institutions would not be as strong centers of research and teaching as they are today.

The Chain Reaction of Federal Programs

To some extent, recent federal programs in higher education have grown out of each other. The GI Bill sent thousands of veterans to college, creating extra strain on college housing facilities. The federal government then helped relieve the strain, first with surplus property disposal to the colleges, and later with the college housing loan program. The National Science Foundation offered fellowships to graduate students in science, allowing them to choose their own place of study. When they tended to collect in a few well-known institutions, the Foundation added the cooperative fellowship program in an effort to distribute the fellowships more widely among institutions and regions. When fellowships and research assistantships open to graduate students in the sciences reduced the supply of able graduate students available for undergraduate teaching, the Foundation set up its program of summer fellowships for teaching assistants. The heavy emphasis on science in the federal programs, plus the concentration of federal funds in universities with strong graduate departments, led to concern about the neglected fields of social science and the humanities and about the development of new centers of graduate study. These twin concerns manifested themselves in the National Defense fellowship program, which not only provided funds for graduate programs in all fields, but specified that programs to be aided must be "new or expanded."

Until recently, the federal government has not subsidized the teaching activities of higher educational institutions directly, except at the land grant colleges. Federal money has gone to students in the form of fellowships, loans, payments for work, or subsistence payments and the students have paid their tuition. Occasionally, as in the World War I program for disabled veterans and in the GI Bill for World War II veterans, the government has paid tuition directly to the institution chosen by the student. Federal money also has gone directly to institutions for special purposes, notably construction and research, but not to pay teaching faculty or the other costs of instruction. This pattern, too, may be changing. Several recent federal programs provide direct support for teaching programs. The National Institutes of Health training grants, the language centers established by the National Defense Education Act, and the National Defense fellowships are the most outstanding examples.

Stipulations for Receiving Federal Funds

Several other trends seem to be discernible in the history of federal relations with colleges and universities. One is that, over the years, the federal government has tended to define more specifically the purposes for which federal funds may be used by colleges and universities which receive them. The grants to new states for state universities did not say what kind of institutions should be established or what should be taught therein. The first Morrill Act specified only that the land grant colleges should teach agriculture, the mechanic arts, and military tactics and should not exclude "other scientific and classical studies." The second Morrill Act was only a little more definite. The federal government did not attempt to review the college programs or to spell out what courses should be taught.

By contrast, several more recent federal programs require the participating institutions to describe in considerable detail the instruction they will offer in a particular field of study. This is true of the National Institutes of Health training grants, for example, and the National Defense fellowships. Under the latter, an institution must describe in detail the graduate program it will offer if federal support is forthcoming and must show that this program will involve new staff or facilities. To be sure, the legislation allows the universities to submit proposals in a wide variety of fields, but decisions on which ones will be supported in which institutions are made by the government prior to the grants, not by the institutions after they receive the money.

In the case of research, the allocation of federal funds for specific projects approved in advance is a firmly established tradition dating from the early days of federal support for research in agriculture. In recent years, some people in universities have been disturbed by the fact that final decisions on large parts of their research programs are made outside the universities and have called for unrestricted federal research grants. As a result, both the National Science Foundation and the National Institutes of Health have started programs of institutional grants, designed to give the universities some undesignated funds for science in addition to project money. It is too soon to say whether this indicates a real trend away from the project system.

The tendency of the federal government to direct its aid to specifically defined types of education does not apply to undergraduate students. Graduate fellowships have been offered only for study in specific fields, but undergraduates eligible for federal assistance have not been required to state in advance what they will study. Students participating in the work-study programs of the

National Youth Administration could take any courses they desired —so far as the federal government was concerned—and the same was true of veterans eligible for benefits under the GI Bill. Under the National Defense student loan program, preference is given to the student who shows certain abilities or who says he intends to teach, but he is not required to state in advance what he will study if he gets the loan.

Participation in Federal Programs

Another marked historical trend has been the inclusion of more and more institutions in the federal programs over the years. Almost all of the approximately 1,900 colleges and universities in the United States now participate in some federal program—be it research, student loans, fellowships, housing loans, or something else —although the amounts of money involved are small for most institutions. The distribution of federal funds is very uneven, but it is also very wide.

Unlike the federal land grants for state universities, the Morrill Act grants were followed by further contacts with the land grant colleges. Not only were there federal contributions to the colleges' operating budgets but also the colleges were used to carry out federal programs of agricultural research and extension and officer training. For many years, the land grant colleges were the only institutions of higher education which had important contacts with the federal government.

After World War I, the group of institutions with federal contacts began to expand. Other institutions, including a few private ones, established ROTC units. Federally sponsored research began to appear in areas other than agriculture and in institutions other than land grant colleges. But the big change came in the 1930's with the advent of federal support for students. The students of all non-profit institutions of higher education, public and private, were eligible to participate in the National Youth Administration work-study program. For most institutions, this was their first substantial involvement with the federal government.

The GI Bill of Rights was even broader. The eligible veteran could use his benefits at any institution approved by his state or the Veterans Administration, even a profit-making one. The government's experience with profit-making institutions under the GI Bill was not very satisfactory—some of them seemed to be trying to make their profit primarily off the government—and they were not included in the National Defense Education Act. Participation in the National Defense student loan program is limited to "public or other nonprofit" institutions which offer at least two years of work acceptable for credit toward a bachelor's degree. Proprietary business schools have lobbied hard, but so far unsuccessfully, for inclusion.

Many private higher educational institutions are affiliated with churches, and the inclusion of private colleges and universities in federal programs has raised some problems about the separation of church and state. No one has seriously questioned the constitutionality of federal aid when the aid goes directly to students as in the GI Bill, or even when it goes to colleges for the sole purpose of helping students, as in the National Defense student loan fund. Nor has anyone seriously questioned, on constitutional grounds, federal support of scientific research in church-related institutions or the provision of federal funds for specifically defined teaching programs in science and languages at these institutions. Presumably, government support for these programs does not contribute directly to the propagation of religious doctrine.

Questions have been raised, however, with respect to the constitutionality of federal support for building programs at church-related institutions. The federal building programs of the 1930's were public works programs, and private colleges and universities were not included. The college housing loan program, begun in 1950, however, extends to all institutions—public and private, including church-affiliated colleges—except independent theological schools. The fact that it is a loan program and a housing program has allayed most fears about its constitutionality. The federal government is subsidizing college building only to the extent that colleges can borrow at less than the market rate of interest. In any case, subsidizing the places where students live and eat seems more like aiding students than aiding church-related institutions.

Those who fear that any federal funds devoted to education inevitably bring federal control of the content and methods of instruction find little support for their position in the history of federal aid to colleges and universities. This does not mean that the federal programs have been free from all difficulties for the participating institutions. Colleges and universities have often complained about federal "red tape," such as the necessity of filling out long and complicated forms before spending federal money, and of making frequent reports to the government on the number of veterans in attendance or the exact disposition of equipment acquired in connection with a research contract. There has been considerable friction between the institutions and the government over payments designed to cover the cost of federal programs when "cost" was open to several interpretations. In many cases, this friction could have been reduced by agreeing in advance on a simple formula which seems fair on the average, rather than negotiating in each individual case. For example, making a flat payment to the college for each graduate student holding a National Defense fellowship would be much more sensible than negotiating to determine the cost of each student's education.

There have also been complaints from some of these institutions that the availability of federal money for scientific research was distorting curricula and keeping their best men away from teaching—but most institutions have not been sufficiently upset about this to stop applying for federal funds. There have been complaints about the distribution of federal money—especially the concentration of research money in a small number of large institutions—and there has been some concern about the loyalty oaths required of students receiving aid, particularly about the affidavit required of borrowers from the National Defense student loan fund. Nevertheless, despite these various sources of difficulty, the colleges and universities involved have, in the main, been well-pleased with the administration of federal programs and have not felt themselves subject to federal dictation. The programs have not brought federal control over the selection of faculty, the content of courses, the choice of text books, or the conclusions of research. Academic freedom has suffered far less at the hands of the federal government than at the hands of many state legislatures and state investigating committees.

To sum up, in spite of the fact that Congress has never explicitly adopted a policy of supporting higher education, federal legislation has profoundly affected the development of our higher educational system. Federal actions have stimulated the foundation of universities and colleges, and the federal government has used the existing educational system to carry out a variety of programs thought to be in the national interest. Some of these programs have put strains on colleges and universities which Congress has attempted to alleviate with other programs. The result has been the gradual development of a whole complex of federal activities affecting both students and institutions of higher education in a variety of ways. This complex was not planned; it just grew. Over the years, the variety of activities for which federal funds are available has greatly increased, and increasing numbers of institutions have become involved.

There are definite signs that Congress is beginning to look on higher education as a national concern and a fit subject for federal legislation in its own right. It, therefore, seems important to turn to the question of what role, if any, the federal government should play in financing higher education. Should the present hodgepodge of federal activities be replaced by a more comprehensive program of aid for higher education? If so, what kind of program should it be?

8

The Case for Government Subsidies to Higher Education

THE COSTS OF HIGHER EDUCATION may be met from three main sources. Funds can come from students and their parents through payment of tuition and fees; or from federal, state, and local governments through subsidies paid to students or to institutions of higher education; or from private philanthropy. The last named has been a comparatively small source of current income to higher educational institutions as a whole in recent years. Moreover, private philanthropy is by definition voluntary. It depends on the goodwill of donors and the effort institutions put into fund raising, although it can be influenced indirectly by changes in the tax laws.[1] Private giving should not be ruled out as a source of funds for higher education, but by far the most important issue to be decided by the institutions and the public is the way in which the burden of support for higher education should be shared between the consumers of education and the tax-paying public.

In 1957-58, the last year for which estimates are available, higher educational institutions combined received 25 per cent of their educational and general income from student tuition and fees; 34 per cent from state and local governments; 19 per cent from the

---

[1] The deduction of gifts to nonprofit educational institutions from individual and corporate income for tax purposes and the exemption of these institutions themselves from most taxes are important forms of public support for higher education which have not been dealt with in this study.

federal government; 14 per cent from endowment and private gifts; and the remaining 8 per cent from a variety of other sources.[2]

Income for educational and general purposes includes income for research and certain other activities not directly related to the instruction of students. For some purposes, it is useful to exclude research and these other activities and look at "income for student higher education" by sources (see Table XVIII). The federal

TABLE XVIII. *Sources of Support for Student Higher Education in Colleges and Universities, 1957-58*

Source	Per Cent of Total
Tuition and fees	36
Gifts and endowment earnings	15
Government	46
State and local	(42)
Federal	(4)
Other	3

SOURCE: Selma J. Mushkin, "Note on Expenditures and Income of Colleges and Universities for 'Student Higher Education,' 1970-75," U.S. Office of Education, *The Economics of Higher Education* (forthcoming). "Student higher education" excludes research, nondegree credit extension work, and student aid.

government does not loom so large as a supporter of higher education when research is excluded, while the importance of state and local government and student tuition and fees is increased.

This chapter seeks answers to two basic questions: Why should any level of government—be it federal, state, or local—subsidize higher education? Why should the federal government play a role in subsidizing higher education? In chapter 9, the advantages and disadvantages of particular methods of federal support will be considered.

The United States and the states and local communities have a

[2] Henry G. Badger, "Higher Education Finances: 1955-56 and 1957-58," *Higher Education*, March 1960, p. 10.

long history of mixed private and public support of higher education. Obviously, we are not going to scrap the whole system and start anew. A shift to complete reliance on private spending would not be politically feasible, even if this were thought to be desirable for economic or other reasons. Nevertheless, it is important to re-examine the basic rationale for public support of higher education as a background for decisions as to how the rising costs of higher education should be shared between students and the public. It is especially important to identify the objectives of public support, because the different objectives imply radically different types of subsidies to different kinds and levels of education.

The Case Against Subsidies

A few economists and educators take the position that higher education need not, and should not, be subsidized. Rather, it should be sold to students at a price sufficient to cover the costs of producing it.[3] In its most extreme form, their argument runs something like this: Higher education is just one of the many commodities and services produced and consumed in the economy. It is a consumer's good, bought for its own sake, like ice cream; and it is also an investment good, bought to increase the future productivity of the purchaser, like machinery. In general, the American system allows producers to produce whatever commodities they expect to yield the greatest profit; investors to invest where they expect to obtain the greatest return; and consumers to spend their money as they choose. We perpetuate this system, not only because we value freedom of choice per se, but also because we have good

---

[3] For a strong statement of this position see B. A. Rogge, "What Price Education," *Wall Street Journal*, May 1, 1959, p. 10, and "Financing Higher Education," *Wall Street Journal*, May 4, 1959, p. 12. For the economic rationale see Milton Friedman, "The Role of Government in Education," in Robert A. Solo (ed.), *Economics and the Public Interest*, Rutgers University Press, 1955; J. Wiseman, "The Economics of Education," *Scottish Journal of Political Economy*, February 1959, pp. 48-58; Ernest Van den Haag, *Education as an Industry*, Augustus M. Kelley, 1956. These three economists admit that society might have reasons for subsidizing nonvocational higher education.

reason to believe that the system leads to maximum production and satisfaction of consumer wants. Government controls or subsidies, or even government operation of some enterprises, may be justified under certain circumstances, but the burden of proof is always on those who allege that interference with the basic system is necessary and desirable.

Those who oppose subsidies for higher education just are not convinced that there is anything special about higher education which justifies its subsidization. They would make loan funds available and urge students to invest in their own higher education as long as the prospect of increasing their future earnings makes such investment attractive to them. In other words, they would rely on the ordinary incentives of the market place to induce people to invest in education to the extent that such investment promised at least as great a return as investment in physical capital goods. They see no reason for using a subsidy to favor educational investment over other types of investment, or for encouraging consumers to spend their incomes on higher education rather than on other consumer goods by selling education to them at less than its cost.

Arguments for Subsidy

The arguments for subsidization of higher education fall into three categories, which might loosely be called "social justice" arguments, "economic growth" arguments, and "national interest" arguments.

Social Justice

The social justice argument is that society owes every individual at least a minimum chance to develop his own capacities. It may be desirable to force adults to rely on their own abilities, but it is manifestly unfair that some children are presented with ample opportunities for self-development and others, through no fault of their own, have little or no chance. The unfairness cannot be eliminated without impairing the incentive of parents to provide for their children, but it can be mitigated by seeing that all children have enough to eat and wear and access to an education. This is the philosophy of school-lunch programs and aid to dependent children and, in part at least, of our whole system of free public education.

The main disagreement here, of course, is over how far the subsidization of education should go. At what point should society say to its children: "All right, we have given you an education up to this level and from now on you are on your own?" The last 50 years have seen general acceptance of the idea that every child has a right to a free high school education in his own community. The question now is to what extent this right also should apply to higher education.

Some would argue that there would be no serious injustice in charging all college students tuition sufficient to cover the full costs of their education. After all, college students are old enough to work and have prospects of good earnings after graduation. Able students whose parents cannot afford to send them to college can work their way through or borrow the money or both, and they will be better off in the end for having learned to rely on themselves and not on the government. Holders of this general point of view often support government loans to students or student work programs sponsored by the government in preference to scholarships or subsidies to institutions.

On the other side, many would argue that even the provision of free public education at the college level is not enough to ensure low-income children an equal chance to develop their capacities. The student who has to earn his room and board is at a disadvantage scholastically. Many low-income families put pressure on children to quit high school and start contributing, not only to their own support, but to the family budget as well. Those who hold this view tend to favor free community colleges located within commuting distance for most students, government scholarships and fellowships covering living expenses, and guidance programs to encourage low-income students to take advantage of these opportunities.

Disagreement on these points grows partly out of basic philosophical differences on the desirable role of the state in a free society, and here no appeal to empirical evidence is really possible. There are some factual questions which are relevant to this discussion but, unfortunately, it is difficult to obtain clear answers. It would certainly be useful to know how many students with the capacity to profit from higher education are now prevented from obtaining it by economic barriers.

Several studies have been made in the past few years to discover what happens to high school seniors after they graduate—which ones go on to college and which do not.[4] These studies have not provided much direct evidence on how college-going is related to ability to pay for education. They have, however, provided a great deal of indirect evidence by showing how college-going is related to the father's education and other things which are closely related to income. The results are not surprising. They show that even students with excellent high school grades and ability-test scores are much more likely to go on to college if their fathers are in professional, technical, or managerial occupations than if they are farmers or laborers. They are more likely to go to college if their parents are well-educated and if they live within commuting distance of a college. Of those who rank in the top third of their class on ability tests—and so may be presumed capable of doing college work—between a third and a half do not go on to college. This "lost talent" is concentrated in poorly educated blue-collar families, presumably many of them in the lower-income group. Moreover, much talent is lost even earlier. Students from poor backgrounds score lower on tests and do poorer work in high school, even though it can often be shown (after special remedial work) that their native intelligence is high.

These facts are well-known, but there is little agreement on their implications. Do they mean that greater subsidies in the form of increased scholarships or more tax-supported colleges are needed

[4] See, for example, Educational Testing Service, *Background Factors Relating to College Plans and College Enrollment Among Public High School Seniors,* Princeton, Educational Testing Service, April 1957, processed; J. Kenneth Little, *Explorations into the College Plans and Experiences of High School Graduates: A State-Wide Inquiry,* University of Wisconsin, School of Education, September 1959; Wendell W. Wright and Christian W. Jung, "Why Capable High School Students Do Not Continue Their Schooling," *Bulletin of the School of Education,* Indiana University, January 1959.

to equalize opportunities for higher education and get talented low-income students into college? Some of the high-ability students who do not go to college are girls who are getting married. Others are boys and girls who want to go into occupations for which college training is not necessary. Many of these say they would have gone to college if they had had the money. However, they may be partly rationalizing, since many of the same students seem to have made little effort to find out about scholarships or loans for which they might have qualified. This leads some observers to believe that scholarships and low tuition alone will not draw these students into college. Their families have not taught them to value education or to make sacrifices to get it, and by the time they finish high school it is already too late to change their basic values. The students may not even be aware of their own abilities. This thinking is reflected in the National Defense Education Act's provisions for federal assistance to state guidance and testing programs in high schools.

Economic Growth

Another case for subsidizing higher education can be based on the relation of education to productivity and economic growth. The basic argument is that education increases the individual's capacity to produce. He decides to devote time and other resources which he could be enjoying currently to getting an education so that he will be better able to produce later. When he does that, he is investing in himself in the same sense that a manufacturer is investing when he devotes current resources to building a new factory. The trouble is that the benefits of educational investment may not accrue to the individual who makes it. Some of the benefits may go to other people. Hence, the individual may not have an incentive to carry his investment in himself to the point at which the return to society on this investment is equal to the return on other expenditures of the same resources. Under such circumstances, society as a whole may gain by taxing resources away from some relatively unproductive use and subsidizing investment in higher education.

The economic benefits of education to society may also come in the form of the avoidance of certain costs. This argument is often used to support public subsidies of elementary and even secondary education. Where any substantial part of the population is poorly educated, crime, disease, and dependency rates tend to be high; unless citizens have some basic education, it is difficult for the government to communicate ideas and to carry out its functions. It is not so clear that there are social costs associated with lack of higher education. But it is clear that highly educated people may make positive contributions to economic growth from which society reaps much of the benefits. They have ideas, do research, make discoveries, invent new products and processes and procedures. Usually, anyone can use these basic ideas and discoveries. It is because their originator may get little or none of the increase in income which they create that not enough people may be induced to invest in the expensive education which this kind of creative activity requires.

Here, again, is an argument which could be elucidated by an appeal to the facts if facts were available, but unfortunately there is very little precise information about the effect of education on income—either personal or national. However, some estimates have been made of the average lifetime incomes of persons with varying degrees of education. These indicate that, at 1958 levels, the lifetime income of the average male college graduate was about $177,000 more (before taxes) than the lifetime income of the average man who graduated from high school, but did not go beyond.[5] This $177,000 income is far greater than the full cost of a college education—even including all the costs to the college, only part of which are normally covered by tuition, and the cost of the lost income which the student might have earned if he had not been studying. But this figure does not tell us whether the education is as profitable as other investments society might make of the same resources.

The difference in income between high school and college graduates occurs not only because the college graduates earn more.

[5] Herman P. Miller, "Annual and Life-time Income in Relation to Education: 1939-59," *American Economic Review*, December 1960, pp. 962-68. See also H. S. Houthakker, "Education and Income," *Review of Economics and Statistics*, February 1959, pp. 24-28.

It also is because they have higher property incomes, at least part of which must be attributed to advantages their families can give them. Similarly, the difference in lifetime earnings is at least partly because the average college graduate is more likely to come from a family that can give him a start in a business or profession. Since he probably is more intelligent, and perhaps more ambitious, than the average high school graduate, the chances are that he would have made more money even if he had not gone to college. Moreover, the earnings of the college graduate are concentrated farther in the future than those of the high school graduate. Other things being equal, an investment which is expected to yield a certain sum in the near future is preferable to one which is expected to yield the same sum at a more distant time.

At least one attempt has been made to allow for some of these differences and compute a rate of return on investment in college education which can be roughly compared with rates of return on other forms of investment. Using 1950 data, Gary S. Becker estimated, adjusting for differences in ability and certain other things, the increase in average lifetime income of urban white males that was reasonably attributable to a college education. The increase, he found, is approximately equivalent to a rate of return of 9 per cent on the total costs of such an education (including the lost income of the student).[6] This is not a startlingly high return, but it does indicate that going to college would have been a pretty good investment for the average urban white graduate even if he had to pay the full costs himself. The return for other males is probably somewhat lower, and it is not at all clear how one would go about including women in this computation.

This type of computation is interesting, though of little help in determining the desirable level of subsidies for higher education. Assume that all subsidies were withdrawn and loan funds made available to students at some interest rate less than 9 per cent. At first glance, it would seem that approximately the same number of men would go to college as at present, since they could borrow the money and still expect to make a profit on the investment. The

[6] Becker, "Underinvestment in College Education?" *American Economic Review*, May 1960, p. 348.

result might be quite different, however. Among other things, 18-year-olds may not be that farsighted—even if they are willing to expose themselves to the risks involved in borrowing. Reducing the present level of subsidies might well reduce the proportion of boys going to college very substantially, even though a detached observer could demonstrate, after the fact, that this development tended to reduce their average income.

Such a computation also fails to indicate the rate of return society as a whole is getting on its investment in higher education and whether additional subsidized investment would be profitable. If the return to society, as reflected in national income, is substantially greater than the return to the individual, then society as a whole may benefit from encouraging this type of investment through subsidies. Unfortunately—although it is easy to point to highly educated people who have made important contributions to national income for which they received little personal remuneration—no one has developed a method of estimating the total return that society is getting, or might get, on its investments in higher education.

The National Interest

Not all of the benefits to society resulting from the support of higher education would show up in the growth of national income. It may be that adequate national defense requires greater expenditures on higher education than would be made by individuals acting in their own self-interest without subsidy from the government. Many people apparently came to this conclusion at the time of the first Sputnik. They reasoned that national survival required us to keep ahead of the Soviet Union in scientific and technological developments and that Russian superiority in rocketry demonstrated that we were not doing so. Apparently, our educational system was not turning out enough good scientists and engineers at prevailing levels of subsidization, and further subsidies were necessary to induce more bright people to educate themselves in science and technology. This type of reasoning has been largely responsible for the recent expansion of federally supported graduate fellowship programs in the sciences.

Similarly, one might argue that highly educated people make contributions to national culture and the quality of national life for which they do not receive adequate remuneration. Although these contributions do not necessarily increase national income, they are nevertheless valuable, and the nation should encourage them by subsidizing higher education. This is not just another way of saying that education is part of the good life—like air conditioning and beer and pretzels. Rather, the argument is that there are special reasons for subsidizing education on the grounds that the contributions educated people make can often be enjoyed by others without charge, and, hence, that a system which relies on producers selling for profit and consumers spending as they choose will not produce as much higher education as society really wants.

While the social justice argument seems to imply the desirability of subsidizing the higher educational process itself, the arguments based on economic growth and national interest may simply indicate the desirability of subsidizing certain activities in which educated people engage. Take scientific research, for example. There are good reasons for thinking basic scientific research should be subsidized. It is needed for national security. Also it is needed because private firms are unlikely to risk their own or borrowed funds in the search for basic knowledge which they cannot appropriate to themselves and sell, even though collectively and eventually they may benefit very greatly from such investment. These are arguments for the government's subsidizing basic research, but not necessarily for its subsidizing the education of basic researchers. The scientist cannot sell the fruits of basic research, but he can sell his own services to the highest bidder as easily as a movie star or a certified public accountant. Assume that basic research is actually subsidized up to the point at which the returns to society on additional investment in basic research are no greater than the returns on other forms of investment. The salaries paid to scientists would have to be high enough to induce the desired number of people to train themselves for this kind of work. If the salaries offered sufficient inducement, there would be no more reason for paying people to take courses in science than for paying them to take courses in law or business or interior decorating.

Part of the subsidy to science might be put into graduate fellow-ships for science students in the belief that this was a quicker, and ultimately cheaper, way of inducing able people to become scientists than relying on increased scientific salaries. This belief would be confirmed if young people were better informed about the fellowships than about income opportunities generally, or if young people valued present benefits, relative to future prospects, more highly than do other people. In the short run, it is certainly easier to inform potential students about fellowship opportunities than about increases in future salary levels. Relying on salary incentives to induce students to train themselves for science would probably take longer than offering fellowships even if the salary increases were well advertised. However, there is no certainty that young people actually value immediate gains more highly than other people do.

There is at least one possible danger in subsidizing education as a means of attracting people to specific professions, rather than making the professions more attractive through increasing the remuneration. The fellowship money can be largely wasted if it goes to students who take the training, and then find the profession unrewarding and go into something else. This possibility has often led legislative bodies to attach conditions to the acceptance of government fellowships or scholarships, usually obligating the student to repay the money unless he enters a specific profession. An example is the National Defense student loan program which provides that up to half of a student's loan will be forgiven if he teaches in a public school. Several states have similar programs under which loans become gifts if the borrower goes into teaching or medicine.

The Risk of Investments in Higher Education

The riskiness of investing in human beings is one other feature of higher education which may justify special treatment. Even those who regard subsidization of higher education as unnecessary and favor raising tuition to, or at least closer to, the full cost of educating a student recognize this problem. Private profit incentives may lead to underinvestment in higher education, owing to the peculiar nature of the risks of such investment—both for the borrower and the lender. Special measures are needed to increase the availability of student loan funds and to make borrowing an acceptable means of financing a college or professional education, just as it is an acceptable means of financing other types of long-term investment.

The Risks for Borrowers and Lenders

The risks for the lender seem obvious. A student may seem capable of earning a good income in an occupation for which education is required, and thus seem to be a good prospect for an educational loan, but there is nothing to ensure that he will use his capabilities. He may decide to be a "bum," and if he does there is very little the lender can do about it. If the loan were for some sort of physical investment, the lender could foreclose on the borrower and at least end up with machines or a factory which he could sell or operate himself. If he lends to a student who fails to use his acquired knowledge, the lender probably ends up with nothing. Hence, lenders may charge especially high interest rates on loans to students or may be reluctant to lend to them at all when less risky alternatives are available.

For these reasons, the advocates of large-scale student borrowing say, it may be necessary for the government to encourage investment in higher education by guaranteeing private loans or by lending students public funds. This need not be costly to the government. Perhaps commercial lenders have overestimated the real risks of lending to students. College graduates have many reasons for wanting to earn income and pay their debts, and past experience with lending to college students has shown them to be good risks. Guaranteeing private loans to students might cost the government virtually nothing, and a public corporation might be able to borrow funds in the market and lend to students at moderate rates without losing money. If this experience shows that students are good risks, commercial lenders might eventually begin competing for the student loan business.

Coping with the borrower's risk is more difficult. The lender, unless he is engaged in a charitable activity, will tend to charge an interest rate which will compensate him for the risk of the borrower's defaulting. If he is lending to a group of students of substantially the same characteristics, he cannot predict which ones will be the defaulters, but he does not really care. He is protected not only by the interest rate but also by the fact that he is lending to a large number of people. The borrower, however, does care. Even if the risk of defaulting appears to be small enough so that he can borrow at a low rate of interest, the student may be reluctant to expose himself even to a small chance that he will not be able to pay off the loan. Defaulting on the loan would mean serious embarrassment for him, though only a relatively small loss to the lender.

A Risk-Pooling Scheme

Several economists have suggested that students be allowed to borrow enough to pay for their education, and to repay some fixed percentage of their annual income, instead of the exact sum borrowed. Milton Friedman has outlined the following plan:

> A governmental body could offer to finance or help finance the training of any individual who could meet minimum quality standards by making available not more than a limited sum per year for not more than a specified number of years, provided it was spent on securing training at a recognized institution. The individual would agree in return to pay to the government in each future year X per cent of his earnings in excess of Y dollars for each $1,000 that he gets in this way. This payment could easily be combined with payment of income tax and so involve a minimum of additional administrative expense. The base sum, $Y, should be set equal to estimated average—or perhaps modal—earnings without the specialized training; the fraction of earnings paid, X, should be calculated so as to make the whole project self-financing.[7]

This intriguing idea shifts the burden of paying for higher education onto those who presumably reap the primary benefit. Never-

[7] Friedman, "The Role of Government in Education," *op. cit.* Similar suggestions have been made by Seymour Harris and William Vickrey.

theless, there would be some serious problems. Participation in the plan would presumably have to be voluntary. Compulsory participation would amount to a special income tax paid only by educated people. This would tend to discourage some types of educational expenditures, and it would be about as politically acceptable as a tax on motherhood or patriotism.

If participation were voluntary, and the exemption and repayment rates were the same for everybody meeting the minimum standards, students who thought they had a good chance of earning incomes above the average for college graduates probably would not participate. Instead, they would try to get a fixed-payment loan from a regular lending agency. Many of these same students would come from families who had incomes high enough to pay the full cost of their children's education, or assets against which they could borrow.

On the other hand, students who did not anticipate high earnings, but wanted to go to college, might well be attracted by the plan. These would include women who did not expect to work after marriage, Negroes and others who feared job discrimination, people who wanted to go into low-income occupations like the ministry, or for other reasons had low estimates of future earning capacity. Many of these would come from families with low incomes or families which had decided to use their limited resources on the education of other children with higher income prospects. Families would tend to borrow under the plan for their daughters, but not for their sons.

This kind of self-selection would not matter if students were poor predictors of their future positions in the income distribution. Actually, they would probably turn out to be reasonably good predictors, especially if they had help from experienced high school guidance officers. It appears likely that an experienced person could do a reasonably successful job of forecasting in which quarter of the lifetime income distribution a student would end, if he knew the student's sex, race, intelligence, high school record, and educational and occupational plans. If so, then those who did participate in the borrowing plan would actually have low lifetime incomes on the average. And if the scheme were to be self-financing, they would be required to pay back a fairly substantial portion of their lifetime earnings. As a result, many of these students might not go to college at all.

The trouble lies in the fact that some individuals are better risks than others. A noncompulsory risk-pooling scheme in which everyone enters on the same terms cannot work well unless the risks being pooled are substantially the same. If the risks are known to be different, then the low-risk people will either succeed in getting more favorable terms for themselves or will get out of the pool and form a new one.

There are two alternatives for a noncompulsory system of lending rather substantial sums to students and having them repay out of future income. Either the students with better prospects will have to be allowed to borrow on better terms than others, or the scheme will have to be subsidized heavily enough to be able to lend to students with relatively poor prospects on terms which are still attractive to those with good prospects. This is equally true whether the individual student is required to repay the exact sum borrowed with interest, or as a percentage of his actual income.

From a purely economic point of view, it might be desirable for students with better income prospects to borrow on more favorable terms. This would help channel educational investment toward students who seemed likely to make the largest contributions to national income. However, an individual's income prospects are not entirely determined by his innate ability, but also by social background and the size of his family's income. These things affect his performance on intelligence tests and the ease with which he can get started in a job or profession. Charging tuition equal to cost, and then lending to people with high-income prospects on more favorable terms, might contribute to the rigidity of the social structure, and make it more difficult for young people from disadvantaged groups to improve their earning capacity by education. In the long run, this would not be a healthy thing for a democratic society—economically or in other ways. The problem is somewhat analogous with one frequently raised by small corporations. Owners allege that they are unable to borrow on terms as favorable as those enjoyed by big corporations, and that this keeps their corporations small and prevents them from competing with the big corporations to the ultimate benefit of consumers.

Which Levels Should Be Most Heavily Subsidized?

At least on grounds of social justice, the case for subsidizing undergraduate education seems much stronger than the case for subsidizing graduate and professional education. As society becomes increasingly technical and complicated, advancement up the social and economic ladder necessarily requires increasingly higher levels of education. When high school education was made freely available to all young people in the early years of this century, sons and daughters of the poor were given an opportunity—perhaps not equal to that enjoyed by the children of the rich, but still a very significant opportunity—to raise themselves well above the general educational level. They had a chance to enter into a variety of high-status occupations for which high school education was then required. This is no longer enough. Almost everybody now goes to high school and almost all jobs require high school training. A college education is now required to get a better than average job and to move up the social ladder. If college education is not subsidized, young people from low-income groups seeking social advancement will find themselves at a greater relative disadvantage than did their counterparts two generations ago, and increased social rigidity will result.

This does not necessarily mean that colleges need to be subsidized in the same way as high schools; there would be no need to provide free public higher education to all would-be students. Social justice certainly does not demand that society subsidize the college attendance of students who are either unable or do not have the self-discipline to profit from a college education. High scholastic standards are not incompatible with equal opportunity, provided care is taken to identify and help talented students whose real abilities may be masked by poor home environment or inadequate schooling at an earlier level.

Nor does the goal of eliminating economic barriers to higher education for talented young people necessarily imply the provision of free higher education for all qualified students. Many students can afford to pay part of the costs of their education and will do so by enrolling in private institutions, even if free public higher education is available. Many people would not object to public institutions shifting part of the burden of paying for higher education onto the primary beneficiaries by charging moderate tuition, provided scholarships as well as loans are available to those who would have real difficulty paying the tuition. Able students who need it should be able to get financial assistance toward living expenses as well as funds to cover tuition.

There are differences of opinion as to what constitutes "moderate tuition." At present income levels, $400 to $500 a year would not seem an excessive charge by a public institution for a full-time student whose family was in the upper half of the income distribution. It would seem appropriate to use both savings plans and loan funds to allow such students and their families to spread the cost of tuition and living expenses over a period longer than four years if they so desire. But student borrowing should not be considered a substitute for scholarships or for subsidies to undergraduate education. It seems likely that many able students in the lower half of the income distribution would not go to college if they had to borrow for even a moderate tuition of $400 or $500 (and perhaps, part or all, of their living expenses), and repay the loan in the conventional manner— even if the interest rate were low. Many able students, especially girls, would be unwilling to take on future liabilities of this magnitude. Hence, loan programs should be supplemented by scholarship programs for students who can show need.

Going beyond undergraduate education, the arguments for asking the advanced professional student to pay a much larger share of the cost (out of borrowed funds, if necessary) seem much stronger. Unlike undergraduate education, this type of education is not designed to raise the general cultural level of the community. Students in law schools, medical schools, graduate schools of business administration, and the like are not there to enhance their general knowledge, or to become better citizens. They are there to prepare for specific careers, from which they expect to reap rewards commensurate with the value of their services to the community.

Moreover, the argument that reliance on borrowing will place insuperable barriers in the path of able students from poor families seems much less cogent at the advanced professional level than at the undergraduate level. A student from a poor family probably would be more willing to borrow if he had completed the under-graduate work with sufficient distinction to gain admission to a recognized graduate or professional school, than if he were starting out as a freshman. He would have more definite plans and would be more sure of his abilities. He would know more about job pros-pects and be better able to predict his approximate future income. Hence, a program of relatively high tuition charges, financed by long-term student borrowing, seems easier to administer at the ad-vanced level than at the undergraduate level. And it is less likely to increase social rigidity by placing insurmountable barriers in the way of able students from low-income groups.

However, even advanced professional students might be reluctant to invest in themselves unless the loans were made available on a long-term basis (20 years or even more), with a moratorium on repayments in the first five years or so. In medicine, for example, almost all graduates can be reasonably certain of earning enough in a lifetime to repay the costs of their medical education, plus interest, without undue hardship. Nevertheless, most young doctors earn relatively little for the first few years after graduation from medical school, while they serve as interns and residents and while they build up a practice. Many would undoubtedly be deterred from borrowing if the loans had to be repaid too soon.

One could argue that much undergraduate education is also mainly professional (undergraduate business education, for ex-ample), and that loan financing is appropriate here, too. However, the line between professional and general education is very hard to draw at the undergraduate level—all courses, even in the liberal arts, contain some mixture of general education and professional training. The reasons for becoming undergraduates in professional schools often are about the same as those of liberal arts undergrad-uates. All undergraduate education probably should be treated as general education, with whatever subsidy is necessary to keep tui-tion charges "moderate" at public institutions and to provide scholarships for able students who need them.

There is also the difficult question of how to treat graduate stu-dents in the arts and sciences. It is tempting to take the position that these students do not really differ from students in law, medical, and other professional schools. They are advanced students preparing for specific careers—primarily in research and college teaching—and they should pay a substantial part of the cost themselves, borrowing on a long-term basis if necessary. It is currently alleged that the expected incomes of college professors and research workers are so far below their true social contribution that most students are unable or unwilling to invest their own funds in these careers. If this is true, then society should take steps to increase the outlook for income in these fields. If the country needs more research botanists or college teachers of Greek, society should accomplish this objective by increasing the attractiveness, pecuniary and otherwise, of these professions, rather than by paying students to take special training and then underpaying them for the rest of their lives. Although tempting, this is not a very realistic position. For one thing, graduate education is produced jointly with, and inseparably from, undergraduate education and basic research. If we are agreed that undergraduate education should receive public subsidies, it is probably neither possible nor desirable to avoid subsidizing graduate education in the arts and sciences as well.

The interaction between graduate education and research is even more obvious. Take, for example, a professor who spends much of his time working with graduate students on research problems and teaching graduate courses closely related to his research interests. Subsidizing this research and compensating him for the time spent on it actually may be equivalent to subsidizing graduate education. A strong argument can be made that strengthening basic research requires strengthening graduate education at the same time and in the same places, not only because this is the way to recruit basic researchers, but because the work itself is best done in a teaching atmosphere.[8] Moreover, where graduate education is a separable activity, it is usually extremely expensive. There are some fields, perhaps vital to the national interest, in which training is so costly, and the number of potential students so small, that no university

[8] For a good statement of this position see The U. S. President's Science Advisory Committee, *Scientific Progress, the Universities and the Federal Government*, November 15, 1960.

could be induced to offer the subject without a government subsidy. Many of the language studies supported by the National Defense Education Act probably fall into this category.

The foregoing are arguments for subsidizing graduate education, but not necessarily for actually paying people to go to graduate school in order to attract them to specific professions. The reasons for doing this are largely pragmatic. It may not be politically feasible to raise salaries in professions like college teaching and research where more able people are thought to be needed, but it may be feasible to get money for fellowships. If this is true, then the fellowship approach is probably better than nothing, but it should be used with caution. In the long run, even if it is possible to attract large numbers of students to graduate school with generous fellowships, the shortage of teachers may not be helped. The students will not stay in the teaching profession unless jobs at sufficiently attractive salaries are available.

The Role of the Federal Government

So far, this discussion has centered on government subsidies, without specifying which level of government should do the subsidizing. It is certainly possible to favor heavy public subsidies to higher education without thinking the federal government should be involved in this process. In fact, most of the past subsidy to higher education has come from state and local governments. Although the federal government has undertaken a variety of programs affecting higher education, except at the high point of the GI Bill of Rights, it has never accounted for a large share of the income of higher educational institutions.

As we have seen, the federal government provided a little less than one-fifth of the educational and general income of colleges and universities in 1957-58. About three-quarters of this was for research, and, as discussed in chapter 3, it is hard to decide how much of this federal research money should be classified as aid to education. A large part goes to research centers where the regular teaching functions of the institutions are affected very little. Much of the rest of the federal research money, however, does help the university perform its teaching functions better, although it does not contribute directly to the institution's budget for instruction. The federal government is presently providing only a very small part of the income of higher educational institutions for purposes other than research. When research is deducted, the federal share of the total is only one twenty-fifth, compared with state and local government contributions of over two-fifths (see Table XVIII). The federal contribution does not include tuition paid by students from federal funds received under the GI Bill and certain fellowship programs, but inclusion of these items would not change the picture significantly.

There are two principal arguments for stepping up federal contributions to higher education in the next decade. One is that the overall needs of higher educational institutions are going to be so great that neither the states nor private individuals will be able to meet them adequately. Hence, the federal government can, and should, act to provide additional resources. The other argument is that certain peculiarly national interests, especially defense, require a shift of resources toward particular types of education, and that this may not happen without action by the federal government.

As noted in chapter 1, the college-age population is increasing rapidly and cost per student can be expected to rise. Unless college-going becomes appreciably more expensive or entrance requirements are raised, between 6 million and 8 million students will be in college by the end of the decade. Costs per student will have to rise if salaries are raised sufficiently to reverse the current trend toward lowering the qualifications of faculty members and to recruit enough new faculty members to carry the increased load. No one knows, of course, exactly how much costs will increase or how many students there will be, but several economists have examined the problem. They have concluded that higher educational institutions will need something in the neighborhood of $10 billion a year for educational and general purposes by 1970 (contrasted with $3.7 billion in 1957-58), and this estimate assumes considerable progress in more efficient use of resources. In other words, an additional

$6 billion or so a year will be needed by 1970.[9] These estimates are based on conservative enrollment projections of around 6 million students by 1970. They assume a doubling of faculty salaries by 1970, but they also assume that the ratio of students to faculty will rise and that ways will be found to cut other costs of instruction. Not included are the estimated $2 billion to $3 billion which will be needed annually for plant expansion by 1970.

Even the more zealous advocates of the need for students and their families to pay a large share of this cost through higher tuition charges admit that some level of government also will have to pay a large share of the increase. Seymour Harris estimates that if fees in public institutions were increased by about three-and-a-half times (to average over $500), and those in private institutions about twofold (to average over $1,100), about $2.9 billion more could come from this source by 1970.[10] In other words, increases of this magnitude would bring in about half the additional $6 billion thought to be needed. However, most people, including Harris, would consider such increases dangerous to equality of opportunity if they were not offset by substantial scholarship programs, presumably paid for largely from public funds. Richard Musgrave regards a general doubling of tuition as probably feasible and estimates this would bring in an additional $2.6 billion at the outside.[11]

State and local governments contributed about $1.2 billion to the educational and general income of higher educational institutions in 1957-58. This was a small item in total state and local budgets (about 3 per cent of current expenditures). No one contends that states and localities could not increase their annual contribution by $3 billion—or even by $6 billion—by 1970, if they chose to allocate an increasing share of their revenues to higher education. But higher education is only one of the many responsibilities of state and local governments and realistically cannot be considered apart from the others.

[9] See Seymour E. Harris, "Broad Issues in Financing," and Robert D. Calkins, "The Role of Government Support" in Dexter M. Keezer (ed.), *Financing Higher Education, 1960-1970*, McGraw-Hill, 1959.

[10] *Ibid.*, p. 75.

[11] Musgrave, "Higher Education and the Federal Budget," *Review of Economics and Statistics*, August 1960 (supplement), p. 96.

There is general agreement that demands for the services performed by state governments are going to increase rapidly in the next decade, probably considerably more so than gross national product. Population growth, and its concentration in the school and retired ages; growing demands for better hospitals and other medical facilities; the motor age and the shift to the suburbs; and the appalling deterioration of central cities—all point to the necessity of rapid expansion in expenditures for education, health, highways, and urban renewal—traditionally areas of primarily state and local activity.[12]

State and local revenues, however, are unlikely to rise fast enough to cover these increased expenditures, unless tax structures are changed or increased aid is forthcoming from the federal government. The problem is that state and local governments depend very heavily on property and sales taxes, rather than on income taxes, which are the main source of revenue for the federal government. Since personal income tax rates are progressive, income tax yields tend to rise considerably faster than income rises. Property and sales tax yields also rise with income, but not nearly as fast as income tax yields do. Property and sales tax rates are usually not progressive; income increases may be spent partly on services or other items not ordinarily covered by a sales tax. Even if property values rise as fast as income, the new values may not be immediately reflected in assessed valuations. Thus, if national income continues to rise, while tax rates remain the same, federal revenues seem likely to increase much faster than state and local revenues.

Approximately two-thirds of the states have income taxes, but major increases in state taxation of income, either corporate or personal, will meet with great opposition, since federal income taxes are already so heavy. Moreover, any individual state will be reluctant to push its tax rates very high for fear that businesses will locate in states with lower tax rates. Hence, there undoubtedly will

[12] See Dick Netzer, "Financial Needs and Resources Over the Next Decade: State and Local Governments," and Gerhard Colm and Manuel Helzner, "Financial Needs and Resources Over the Next Decade at All Levels of Government," in National Bureau of Economic Research, *Public Finances: Needs, Sources and Utilization,* Princeton University Press, 1961.

be pressure from the states for considerable increases in federal grants and contributions.

Higher education presumably will continue to be a relatively small item in state and local budgets, compared to elementary and secondary education. At present, state and local governments appropriate approximately 10 times as much for elementary and secondary education as they do for higher education. One cannot really argue that the states could not afford substantial increases in higher education alone. But one can argue that the states are going to find it impossible to do an adequate job on all fronts without increased federal aid and that, for various reasons, higher education is a peculiarly appropriate area into which to channel the needed funds.

One reason for this is that institutions of higher education within a state serve not only state residents, but out-of-state students as well. Elementary and secondary schools, libraries, hospitals, and a good many other public facilities mainly serve the residents of a limited area; but a large proportion of college students come from other states either in search of better education or just to gain the experience of living in a different part of the country. Most people regard this mixing of college students from different locales as a healthy thing for higher education. And some fear that state legislatures, under pressure of rising enrollments and costs, may wonder why they should educate students from other states, and will make it increasingly difficult and expensive for out-of-state students to attend these institutions.

Not only do college students migrate from one state to another, but also college graduates. The more highly educated a person is the more likely he is to live in a state other than that in which he received his education. Again, this would seem to mark higher education as particularly appropriate for national support.

Another reason for thinking higher education a good place to increase federal support is that considerable experience with different types of federal programs in higher education has already accumulated. By and large, these federal programs have been deemed successful. In particular, there has been little evidence that these programs have brought government control of the type so often feared by opponents of federal programs in education—of dictation of subject matter and textbooks or investigation into the opinions and associations of university personnel. Perhaps for this reason, many of those who oppose federal aid to elementary and secondary education (especially for purposes other than construction), on the grounds that it might bring thought control from Washington, are not similarly concerned about federal aid to higher education.

The special problem of the private colleges and universities—whose costs are rising faster than income from tuition and endowment—also seems to many to make higher education a particularly appropriate area for federal action. If most, or all, of the necessary increase in government funds comes from state governments it will go mainly to public institutions, since almost all of the states are too heavily committed to their public institutions to take on programs of support for private ones. The federal government, however, has a tradition of working both with public and private institutions, and presumably can continue to do so. Perhaps anomalously, this type of reasoning has turned some of the strongest believers in private education into advocates of federal support for higher education in general.

A strong case for federal aid can also be made on the grounds that there are particular educational needs at the national level which may not be apparent to states, localities, and private persons, and which may not be met unless the federal government acts. For example, the close connection between rapid scientific advances and national defense (as well as national health and economic growth) would seem to indicate that the federal government cannot afford to leave scientific education to decision-makers who may not be sufficiently impressed by these national needs or feel any particular responsibility to meet them. If the national interest demands a rapid shift of resources into education for scientific research, then the federal government should encourage this shift by expanding its subsidies to this type of education.

An equally good case of national interest can be made for the importance of training more and better students in foreign languages and cultures and the economic and political problems of other countries. This, again, is a need which is very clear at the national level, but may not be reflected quickly enough in the programs of individual institutions in the absence of federal stimulation.

On a more general level, there is a national interest in reducing the waste of talent attributable to inequality of educational opportunity among students of different income levels and those from different parts of the country. It can be argued that the nation as a whole cannot afford this waste and that the federal government ought to move to eliminate it. Presumably, this implies a federal scholarship program to help intelligent children of low-income families go to college; but it might also imply general subsidies to states or to educational institutions designed to improve the quality of education offered to those who do get to college, especially to improve quality in the poorer states.

The desirability of equalizing the opportunities offered students in rich and poor states and providing all with at least a minimum standard of education has been one of the most frequent arguments in favor of federal aid to education on the elementary and secondary level. It has not figured prominently in debate on federal aid to higher education, although conceivably it should. One reason is that the high proportion of students enrolled in private institutions of higher education in some states makes it difficult to define "equality of opportunity" or "equality of effort." Some states with high per capita incomes (such as New York and Massachusetts) have relatively poor records of support for public higher education, but have relatively large proportions of their college-age population enrolled in institutions supported primarily by private funds. Nevertheless, however one measures them, there are wide disparities in the opportunities for, and quality of, higher education confronting potential students in different states which could be reduced by federal assistance. The recognition that this was true at the graduate level was one of the factors which prompted enactment of the graduate fellowship program of the National Defense Education Act.

To sum up, the federal government probably is going to have to relieve the states of some of their growing fiscal burdens in the next 10 years, and higher education is a particularly appropriate burden for the federal government to relieve. This is because of the relation between education and national security, because of the interstate mobility of college students and graduates, and because of the national interest in reducing the disparity in opportunities for young people from different parts of the country.

It should be emphasized that there is a need for federal support for the actual instructional functions of colleges and universities, in addition to federally sponsored research at higher educational institutions. The latter undoubtedly will, and should, continue to increase, but $1 billion, or even $2 or $3 billion, more in federal research money will not close the gap between anticipated income of colleges and universities and the direct and indirect costs of instructing students. It is true that the magnitude of federally sponsored research is not irrelevant to the size of this gap. In particular, if federal research funds were shifted rapidly from universities to independent research organizations, the universities would have to raise salaries, or provide more research money, or both, in order to hold their best-qualified faculty members. Nevertheless, the issues should not be confused. The magnitude of total federal support for basic research (both in and out of universities) should be determined, insofar as possible, with reference to the needs of the economy and the defense effort, and should not be viewed as aid to higher education.

9

Methods of Federal Aid: Issues to be Resolved

IF FEDERAL AID to higher education is to be substantially increased in the next few years, what form should this aid take? Should it go to colleges and universities directly or should it go to students? If to colleges and universities, should it be earmarked for specific purposes or should the institutions themselves be allowed to decide how to spend the money? If to students, should the federal funds be in the form of loans or scholarships, and should these be awarded on the basis of need or ability or both? Should the students be allowed free choice of field and place of study or should some attempt be made to influence their choice?

These are only some of the difficult and interrelated questions facing those who seek to design a program of future federal activities in higher education. There have been so many proposals in the past few years and so much discussion—some of it more emotional than constructive—that it may be helpful to review the principal issues and to summarize the arguments on each side. The main policy alternatives are listed in Table XIX and the rest of this volume is devoted to discussing these alternatives and considerations relevant to choice among them. Suggestions for a federal program are briefly outlined at the end.

One of the main issues to be resolved is whether the federal government should direct its aid to institutions of higher education or to students, or whether it should do both. The answer to this question depends in part on the primary objective of federal activity in

TABLE XIX. *Federal Aid to Higher Education:*
The Principal Alternatives

A. Aid to institutions.

1. Purposes: construction or instruction or research.

2. Administration:
   a. Block grants or support of specific programs.
   b. Formula distribution (based on enrollment, geography, or other criterion) or evaluation of proposals for use of funds.
   c. Administration by states or other intermediate agencies or direct federal contact with institutions.

3. Participation: public or nonsectarian or all nonprofit or all institutions of higher education.

4. Forms of aid: grants (matched, unmatched) or loans (at the government borrowing rate or at a lower rate) or loan guarantees.

B. Aid to students.

1. Purposes: getting students into college who are not now going or aiding institutions through their students.

2. Administration: by states or institutions (with funds apportioned by formula) or by federal government (with or without geographic or other quotas).

3. Conditions of aid.
   a. Selection on ability or need or other grounds (military service, vocational plans).
   b. Specify fields of study or let student choose after he gets the aid.
   c. Specify institutions or locations or let student choose after he gets aid.

4. Forms of aid: scholarships (flat sum, stipend adjusted to need, or stipend adjusted to cost of institution chosen) or loans or loan guarantees.

C. Integrated support for institutions and students.

1. Support for institutional programs of research and/or teaching under which part of the money can be used for support of students.

2. Scholarship programs with accompanying payments to institutions.

higher education. If the primary objective is to reduce a waste of talent by helping more potential students finance a college education, or to raise scholastic standards in the high schools by offering incentives for academic achievement, then aid to students seems the most logical approach. If, however, the main objective is to strengthen types of education which are related to national defense, or to strengthen higher education generally, then there is much to be said for direct aid to institutions. The argument is that the first requisite of a good educational system is strong educational institutions; that strong institutions need resources; and that if the federal government is going to help provide these resources it should do so in the most direct and obvious way—by making grants or loans to the institutions themselves. Those who favor this approach would not necessarily rule out supplementary programs of federal aid to students, but they do not regard aid to students as a satisfactory substitute for supporting institutions directly.

Aid to Institutions

Given the objective of helping to support higher educational institutions, a number of subsidiary issues must be resolved. One issue which has received considerable attention, in connection both with higher education and with possible federal aid to elementary and secondary schools, is this: Should the federal government limit its aid to the financing of buildings and other physical facilities, or should it support the current operations of educational institutions as well? Many people advocate limiting federal aid to brick-and-mortar programs because they feel that limiting federal support to construction minimizes the danger that the government will exert control over the scope and content of instruction. The need for a new building can be determined by some simple rule of thumb, and Congress seems unlikely to make the receipt of building funds conditional on the acceptance of any federal stipulations about curriculum, content of courses, or beliefs and opinions of faculty and students. Moreover, those who take this position argue, the provision of federal funds for campus buildings also will strengthen instruction, since it will release institutional funds which would otherwise have to be devoted to construction.

On the other side, it is pointed out that buildings do not make a college, and that many colleges find it easier to raise money for such tangible objects as buildings than to find sufficient operating funds. The most urgent and important need of most educational institutions is for funds to pay salaries, and if the federal help is to be effective it should meet this need directly. Those who favor federal support of instructional programs may take either of two positions on federal control. Some may fear federal control, but feel that it is possible to have federal support for instruction without onerous controls—after all the land grant colleges have been receiving such support for some 70 years without evidence of federal dictation. Others may regard certain federal controls as desirable. In particular, they may be distressed by the low academic standards of many institutions, and feel that placing conditions on receipt of federal funds would raise these standards and promote higher levels of scholastic achievement in colleges and universities.

There is also support for focussing federal aid to higher education mainly on research, but using research support as a means of contributing to the general support of the educational institutions concerned. This could be accomplished in three ways: continuing or expanding the present volume of federally financed research at educational institutions; increasing allowances for overhead costs; and making more institutional grants of unrestricted funds, based on the volume of federally supported research at the institution. The argument for this approach is that there is a strong national interest in supporting research and that education—especially graduate education—is so intimately connected with research that it is best supported in conjunction with research. Opponents of this position make the point that strong undergraduate education is at least as important to the nation as graduate education and research, and that most liberal arts colleges and junior colleges (and, indeed, many departments within universities) do little or no research. For them to try to embark on research projects in order to obtain federal support for their other activities would be wasteful, both of their resources and the government's.

Assume for the moment that the federal government is to support the instructional activities of institutions of higher education, presumably in addition to research and certain kinds of construction. Then the important question to be decided is whether the support should be directed toward specified subjects or programs of particular interest to the federal government, or whether it should take the form of block grants to be used at the institution's discretion. This issue is worth examining in some detail.

The Case for Undesignated Federal Grants

A good case can be made for scrapping the whole complicated structure of federal programs in higher education and substituting a system of unrestricted block grants to colleges and universities. The principal argument for undesignated grants is that the colleges themselves are in a better position than either Congress or the federal agencies to assess their needs and to allocate a given amount of subsidy so that it will do the most good for higher education. American colleges and universities are a diverse group of institutions, catering to different types of students, and having different objectives and resources. Many would say that the appropriate role of the federal government is not to influence the curricula or other activities of individual institutions, but to strengthen the whole system by providing subsidies which each institution can use to achieve its particular educational objectives.

Almost without exception, present federal programs provide funds only for specific purposes. It can be argued that the effect of this federal earmarking is to distort college and university programs into patterns the institutions would not themselves have chosen. These distorted programs, it is said, do not reflect the best interests of higher education as seen by the educators—who know most about it. For example, a university may be induced to apply for federal funds to finance a special program in science or languages because such funds are available, although it actually feels its history department or its law school is in greater need of strengthening.

Of course, earmarked federal funds need not lead to significant alterations in college and university activities. If they are earmarked for activities the institutions would have undertaken anyway, they may simply free institutional funds for other purposes. But, in this case, the same result could have been accomplished by undesignated grants. The point is that, whenever federal funds are designated for specific purposes, a certain amount of influence lodges outside the institution, where the decisions made may be less than optimum from the point of view of filling needs most urgently felt on an individual campus.

Precedents for Undesignated Grants

The advocates of block grants can turn for precedent to the annual subsidies which the federal government has paid, since 1890, to the land grant colleges. Although these have never been large, they were an important source of income to many of the colleges as they struggled to get started and gain state support in the early years. To be sure, the grants are not completely undesignated. They can be used only for instruction in "agriculture, the mechanic arts, the English language, and the various branches of mathematical, physical, natural, and economic science. . . ." Within these general areas, however, the colleges have been able to use these grants for whatever current expenses most needed to be met, and there seems to be unanimous agreement that the federal government has refrained from exercising any control over institutional decisions with respect to curricula, standards of admission, hiring of faculty, and the like.

Another frequently cited example of a well-functioning system of undesignated government grants to higher educational institutions is that found in Great Britain. The British universities are private nonprofit corporations, but, over the years, an increasing proportion of their income has been from the government. Over 72 per cent of the total income of British universities, in 1955-56, came from parliamentary grants—the proportion being appreciably lower for Oxford and Cambridge, which have substantial endowments, than at the poorer "provincial" universities and university colleges.[1]

[1] Robert O. Berdahl, *British Universities and the State,* University of California Press, 1959, p. 2 and Appendix IV. For an interesting discussion of the British system, see also, Harold W. Dodds, *et al., Government Assistance to the Universities in Great Britain,* Columbia University Press, 1952.

The British government grants to the universities are administered by a peculiarly British organization called the University Grants Committee, established, in 1919, as a semi-independent arm of the Treasury. This Committee is composed of distinguished scholars in and out of academic life, who, with the exception of the chairman, serve without pay. The Committee works closely with the universities and, after extensive consultation, works out estimates of total university needs for government support in the next five years. These estimates are submitted to the Treasury (which may scale them down) with an accompanying statement of the general objectives to be accomplished, but without any precise indication of how the University Grants Committee intends to allocate the funds. Parliament must vote an annual sum, included in the government's budget, for this purpose, but Parliament is not given access to the financial records of the universities or of the Committee. Also, Parliament cannot reject individual items in the government's budget and would not reject the whole budget because of the university grants. Once a total sum is voted, the University Grants Committee divides it among the individual institutions, employing some informal, never-disclosed allocation procedure, with which, *mirabile dictu,* everyone concerned seems to be reasonably well satisfied.

The University Grants Committee makes both recurrent grants for current operations and nonrecurrent grants for capital expansion. The latter are earmarked for specific building projects; the recipient institution is not allowed to take funds granted for a library wing and use them for a laboratory. The recurrent grants, however, are not earmarked, and the recipient university has a considerable amount of discretion over their use. That this discretion is not unlimited is apparent, however, since the overall program of university activities on which the original estimates of need were based was worked out by the university in close consultation with the University Grants Committee. No institution is likely to risk antagonizing the Committee and jeopardizing its future income by departing substantially from this program without Committee approval.

Immediately after World War II, the University Grants Committee experimented for a few years with earmarking funds for current operations of specific university programs. This was mainly in an effort to encourage university expansion in the sciences, medicine, and certain other professional fields, in which shortages of trained people were felt to be a national concern. After 1952, the earmarked grants were dropped, and the Committee returned to its prewar practice of making block grants, except for capital expansion.

While the University Grants Committee clearly exerts informal, but very substantial, influence on the development of university programs, it has scrupulously avoided any interference with university autonomy in connection with admission of students and hiring and firing of faculty. And it has never concerned itself with the opinions of teachers or the conclusions of research. Academic freedom is highly prized in Britain and has no more zealous guardian than the University Grants Committee.

The Case Against Undesignated Grants

It is hard to conceive of an American Congress turning over the allocation of federal money for higher education to a University Grants Committee. If Congress embarked on a general program of unrestricted subsidies to colleges and universities, it probably would specify in the legislation what types of institutions were to be eligible and how the allocation of funds was to be made. This in itself would be no easy problem. The United States has some 1,900 institutions of higher education, and no set of national qualifications for the title of "college" or "university." Most states grant charters to educational institutions rather freely with no attempt to evaluate the quality of the education offered, although voluntary regional associations of higher educational institutions do exist which impose minimum standards of accreditation on their members. In establishing eligibility requirements for general federal subsidies, the government would have the choice of accepting the verdict of the states or regional accrediting associations, as it has done in the past, or setting up its own accreditation procedure. In any case, to be politically acceptable to Congress, eligibility criteria would probably have to be broad and any allocation system would have to be based on an easily applied formula, such as so much per student.

The opponents of such a program contend that it would be wasteful. Many colleges, even accredited ones, have extremely low standards of admission and achievement; many have such low enrollments that they cannot possibly operate efficiently. Subsidizing some of these would perpetuate inefficiency and mediocrity at federal expense. Moreover, even the "better" institutions might not spend the money wisely. Some might put it into activities for which they were ill-suited or for which adequate facilities already existed. What the institutions considered most urgent might not coincide with even the most liberal interpretation of the national interest.

Another contention is that Congress might impose conditions on the block grants—loyalty checks, for example—and that once this happened the institutions would find they had sacrificed much more autonomy than they would have under a system of earmarked grants and contracts. Under the latter, a university which objects to the conditions attached to federal funds for a particular project, or finds this project unsuited to its overall program, can simply decide not to apply for the money. Such a decision would not endanger its chances of getting federal money for other purposes. Conditions imposed on block grants, however, are harder to resist, since the resisting institution must forego all its federal income.

Critics of a system of block grants also object to the premise on which such a system rests. That is they do not think it is desirable for the federal government to support higher education generally, rather than to foster particular programs of special national importance. Virtually no one in the United States is in favor of the federal government taking over a large share (say, as much as 50 per cent) of the burden of financing higher education. The United States has evolved a system of mixed state and private support and control of higher education, which, by and large, has worked well. If one starts from the position that federal subsidies to higher education should be kept as small as possible, consistent with the national interest, then the relevant question is how comparatively small amounts of federal money can be applied most effectively to accomplish federal objectives. From this point of view, unrestricted grants to all higher educational institutions seem much less attractive than earmarked grants for special purposes.

If federal money is available from a variety of sources and for a variety of purposes—language centers, training programs in science and other crucial areas, research, laboratories, classroom buildings, dormitories—the institutions will have considerable freedom in applying for programs which fit their needs. At the same time, federal agencies will have some latitude in applying their funds where they seem likely to produce the best results. They can make grants to institutions which seem most likely to do high-quality work; they can try to avoid duplication of expensive facilities in the same area, excessive geographical concentration, or uneconomic fragmentation; and they can impose criteria of need on requests for funds for buildings and other purposes. If the federal government were to try to get the same results through a system of unrestricted block grants it would have to take one of two actions. The amount of contributions would have to be increased considerably to cover waste, duplication, and institutional decisions to concentrate on programs of low national priority. Or conditions would have to be imposed on the acceptance of the block grants which would endanger institutional autonomy far more than the conditions attached to earmarked funds.

Grants or Loans?

As an alternative to outright grants to institutions, a system of federal loans has been advocated—mainly on two grounds. Loans are said to be an appropriate way of financing "self-financing" projects and they offer a solution to the difficult church-state issue.

Dormitories and cafeterias, for example, can be made self-financing by charging the students prices sufficient to generate enough revenue to pay off the initial cost with interest over a period of years. Loan financing certainly seems appropriate here. The idea behind such federal lending programs as the College Housing Loan Fund is that the government can facilitate college borrowing by acting as intermediary between colleges and investors who are willing to lend to the government at lower rates than those at which they would lend to the colleges. Whether or not this should be regarded as a "subsidy" is a definitional question (see chapter 5), but it clearly is a use of the powers of the government to channel resources into college building which would otherwise have gone into something else.

There is little sentiment for financing college housing by means of government grants. Even the college housing program has been opposed by some, mainly because they regard the program as an unnecessary invasion of the private capital market. Some of these people would favor shifting to a program under which the government would guarantee private loans to colleges for building projects.

Classrooms, laboratories, and other types of instructional buildings are not directly self-financing, and seem much less appropriate for loan financing. More instructional facilities will allow colleges and universities to enroll more students, but, in general, the tuition paid by these students will not pay the current costs of their instruction, let alone interest and amortization on the facilities they use. Since the financial position of colleges and universities is not expected to improve markedly in the future, there are strong arguments for helping them finance instructional buildings through grants rather than loans. Loans, of course, seem even less appropriate as a means of financing current expenses.

Loans and the Church-State Issue

Part of the support for loans has come from those who would like to see the federal government help all types of public and private colleges, including church-related ones, but who regard grants to church-related institutions as unwise or unconstitutional and loans as an acceptable alternative. The whole question of how far the federal government can go in aiding church-affiliated colleges without impinging on the separation of church and state is surrounded by a legal and conceptual haze. Some people regard the distinction between grants and loans as important, feeling that as long as a church-related college has an obligation to repay a loan with interest it is not really getting government "aid" and hence no constitutional problems arise. Others regard this distinction as immaterial. They feel that if the government uses its power to enable an institution to borrow funds at lower rates of interest than those at which it could borrow on the open market, it is aiding the institution just as significantly as if it were awarding a grant.

In this connection, an alternative distinction which is often drawn is that between general support of church-affiliated educational institutions and support of particular programs at such institutions. Again, some people regard this distinction as important, feeling that aiding science education or language instruction at a church-related college does no violence to the separation of church and state since the money cannot be used for religious indoctrination. Others regard this distinction as unrealistic, pointing out that government support of nonreligious programs releases institutional funds for other purposes, including religious teaching, and may have much the same effect as outright grants for general purposes.

In any case, the existence of church-affiliated colleges and the desire of many people to find ways of helping these colleges without violating the Constitution, or setting a precedent for federal aid to other religious activities, has had considerable impact on the debate about desirable forms of federal aid to higher education. It has strengthened the case of those who favor loans rather than grant support and, consequently, the case of those who favor aid for construction rather than operating expenses. It has also strengthened the case of those who favor earmarked grants rather than undesignated subsidies for operating expenses of higher educational institutions.

Aid for Students

An alternative to aiding institutions, of course, is aiding students by providing them with loans or scholarships or other types of funds with which to pay for their own education. The idea of federal aid for students has become increasingly popular in recent years, as indicated by the program already put into effect and a great many serious proposals for more legislation.

The advocates of federal aid to students have several different things in mind. Some of them view aid to students as a desirable method of subsidizing higher education generally. They point out that direct grants to colleges and universities, whether earmarked or not, involve at least potential danger of federal encroachments on the autonomy of these institutions. When the funds are earmarked for specific purposes, they tend to "distort" institutional programs in favor of these purposes—this is assumed to be bad—and when they are not earmarked Congress may still be tempted to impose conditions and restrictions which will impinge on the freedom of the recipient colleges. If the federal money goes to the students, they argue, the danger of federal control is minimized. In fact, the federal government need have no contact with the institutions at all. It can simply mail checks to the eligible students and let them pay their own way, as do any other students, at the colleges and universities which they choose.

Many of those who advocate federal aid to students as a means of supporting higher education are particularly concerned about preserving the traditionally important place of the private college and university in American life. The argument is that, under present circumstances, the only way the private colleges can survive is by raising tuition well above current levels and closer to the full cost of educating students. But if they do that, they will price themselves out of the market and lose many of their students to the subsidized state colleges and universities, unless the federal government steps in with a program to help students pay for the cost of private higher education. Helping students pay higher tuition fees is also seen as a method of aiding private church-related institutions indirectly without running into any constitutional problems.

The type of federal program which would be of most benefit to private colleges and universities would resemble the original (World War II) GI Bill of Rights. In other words, a large number of students would be eligible; they could study anywhere they could gain admittance; and the federal government would pay customary tuition plus some sort of maintenance allowance. This would be of maximum benefit to private institutions, whose tuition fees cover (or might be raised to cover) a high proportion of their actual costs, but of little help to public institutions, whose fees generally cover only a small fraction of their costs. Of course, public institutions might raise their fees, too, in order to take advantage of the federal program. This would shift part of the burden of subsidizing higher education from the states to the federal government, and it would cause few tears within the private institutions.

A case for federal aid to students can also be made on the grounds that the federal government should take steps to reduce the national waste of talent which occurs because bright children from low-income families are unable to finance a college education. The failure to invest in these children's education, wherever they live, represents a loss to the country as a whole. There are many questions about how to set up a program to help low-income students finance their education. One is the question of how to choose the students. From time to time, there have been unsuccessful attempts to pass legislation giving veterans of peacetime military service benefits similar to the education provisions of the GI Bill of Rights. However, fitness for military service does not necessarily imply fitness for higher education, and such a program would benefit many men who could well afford to pay their own way. And it would exclude most women and all physically handicapped persons.

Another proposal has been a system of national scholarships based solely on ability. Some sort of test of aptitude or achievement, or both, would be administered throughout the country and those who did best—the top X per cent—would receive federal scholarships large enough to enable them to go to college. Proponents of this plan stress that it would be a great stimulus to academic effort in the high schools and that, while unquestionably much of the money would go to students who did not need it, this is better than subjecting the needy students to a degrading "means test."

The main argument against aid based solely on ability is the waste of federal funds involved. Students who score highest on the types of college aptitude tests now in use come heavily from middle and upper-class neighborhoods with good school facilities. Most of these children will go to college anyway. Moreover, the comparatively few low-income children who score in the upper 1 per cent, or 3 or even 5 per cent, on these tests will get scholarships from private sources. The waste of talent is not so much here, as a little lower down the scale in the able-but-not-brilliant group and among those who, because of poor training at home and in schools, do not show their true abilities on a standard test.

If the same amount of federal money were applied to scholarships awarded on the basis of need, rather than on the basis of ability, it would be more effective in enabling students to go to college who could not otherwise go. A means test, however, would make the program more complicated to administer and there might be some stigma attached to holding the scholarships.

A compromise procedure frequently proposed is the following: to administer a nation-wide test and designate the students who scored in the top X per cent as "National Scholars," or some such title. All the National Scholars would receive a token prize, perhaps $100, perhaps more. Additional amounts up to a maximum limit would be awarded (but not announced publicly) on the basis of need. The easiest way to determine need would be to find out the taxable income of the student and his parents or legal guardians, and the number of persons being supported by this income; to refer to an agreed table showing how much a family in these circumstances should be expected to contribute to the higher education of one child; and to award the student the difference between this expected parental contribution and an agreed maximum. The family's liquid assets and other resources could also be taken into consideration, unless it was thought that eliminating a few inequities was not worth the cost of making the administration of the program too complicated.

However the ability-need question might be resolved, there are several other problems which would come up in connection with any program of federal aid to students. One is the problem of geographic distribution. Even if ability is the first criterion of award, there is some argument for ensuring a wide geographic distribution of awardees by taking the top X per cent of the applicants from each state or region. Besides making the program more acceptable to Congress, the theory is that state quotas reduce the handicap imposed on bright students in states with poor school systems. The top X per cent in Mississippi may not score as high as the top X per cent in New York, but perhaps they would have if they had been educated in New York schools. On the other hand, eliminating the geographic quotas may provide more incentive to the areas with poor schools to improve them.

Then there is the question of whether the students should be allowed to go to any college that will accept them, or whether an attempt should be made to influence the distribution of colleges chosen. Selecting students on the basis of ability, and then letting them choose the institutions best suited to their interests, is a procedure with a great deal of appeal. In practice, however, it may result in concentrating the federally aided students in a few well-known schools in a few areas of the country, which may be detrimental to the building of strong institutions in other parts of the country. It may also be more expensive if the student's "need" is based on the cost to him of the institution he wishes to attend. A bright student from a low-income family in central Illinois will probably need about twice as much money to go to Yale as to go to the University of Illinois. It is not clear that the national interest is better served by sending him to Yale, than by using the funds to send him and a second student to state universities near their homes.

One alternative is to give the students aid which can be used only at institutions within their home states. Essentially, this would mean federal financing for state scholarships similar to the present New York State Regents' scholarships which are awarded to New York residents for use at any institution, public or private, in the state of New York. Some might regard this as an undesirable limitation on student mobility. It would certainly lead to peculiar results in such multi-state metropolitan areas as New York and Chicago, where out-of-state students are within commuting distance of urban universities. Presumably, special provision could be made for students who could show cause why they needed to go out of state.[2]

A second alternative is to apportion the federal student aid funds to the institutions themselves on the basis of a formula, and let the institutions pick the students. This is essentially what it now done under the National Defense student loan program, and the same idea might be used for scholarships. One disadvantage is that, especially if students are not allowed to apply to more than one place, there may be great disparities in the abilities of the students aided at different institutions. It would be possible to assign insti-

[2] World War I disabled veterans were required to pick colleges and universities within their general areas, but on a showing of cause could pick institutions anywhere in the country.

tutional quotas on a formula basis, administer a national test, and allow the winners to apply at several places. Then, perhaps, student and institutional preferences could be matched centrally on an electronic computer, as is done with hospital selection of interns.

There is also the question of whether the students aided should be allowed to study anything they wish or whether aid should be offered for study in particular fields. At the undergraduate level, the case for undesignated student aid is very strong. Few entering students have firm ideas about what they want to study, and those who do often change their minds. There seems to be general agreement that offering aid to undergraduates for study in, say, science, would be undesirable, although there is some sentiment for limiting scholarship aid to the liberal arts on the grounds that vocational curricula are more appropriate for loan financing. At the graduate level, it is probably necessary at least to ascertain what field the student intends to enter, since his ability and preparation can only be evaluated intelligently if his field is known. The question here is whether aid should be extended to graduate students in all fields, roughly in proportion to the demand for such aid, or whether an effort should be made to attract students to particular fields by offering disproportionate amounts of aid in certain fields, as is now being done in science.

General Outlines of a Suggested Federal Program

Consideration of all these alternative programs and conflicting points of view on aid to higher education suggests a number of conclusions about the appropriate role of the federal government. They are not startling conclusions. They do not imply scrapping the present structure of federal programs and substituting some bold new approach. On the contrary, they imply that most of the existing federal programs should be continued on an expanded and more permanent basis.

It seems clear that the federal government should plan to increase substantially its support of higher education in the near future. The reasoning behind this position has already been stated:

1) Higher education is an important federal concern from the point of view of economic growth, national defense, and equality of opportunity.

2) The financial needs of higher education are going to rise rapidly in the near future.

3) State and local governments are likely to have increasing difficulty in meeting their financial burdens, and higher education is a particularly appropriate burden for the federal government to assist in relieving.

If the increased federal money is to do any real good, it must be directed toward support of the instructional functions of institutions of higher education. This does not mean that the federal government should stop supporting research in colleges and universities—far from it—but research funds should not be used to cover deficits in institutional budgets for instruction. Research should be supported for its own sake, at a level determined, however inexactly, by national needs for new ideas and discoveries. It should, however, be supported in ways which will strengthen, rather than weaken, the higher education system. Full overhead cost should be paid, and new installations should be located where maximum use can be made of them for teaching as well as research purposes.

Federal funds should also be made available for college and university construction. Such funds meet demonstrable needs of colleges and universities and are relatively easy to administer. The College Housing Loan Fund should be expanded and continued as long as the institutions can show a clear need for additional housing. Research facilities and instructional buildings, such as classrooms and laboratories, also seem particularly appropriate for federal financing. Since these buildings are not self-financing in the sense that dormitories and dining facilities are, federal grants are preferable to subsidized loans. Matching provisions might be useful in encouraging nonfederal contributions. Building grants should be made available to both public and private institutions that can show their present facilities are overcrowded. Loans might be substituted for grants to church-affiliated institutions if the courts find the grants unconstitutional—which seems unlikely—or if the institutions prefer loans to matched grants.

Federal support for teaching functions does not necessarily imply unrestricted block grants to higher educational institutions. It would be preferable to continue to apply federal funds to particular programs of special national importance, but greatly to expand the range of programs supported and the distribution of funds. This would give the federal government the ability to impose some standards, and to put funds for particular programs where they seem most needed and where they seem most likely to be well used. But it also would leave the institutions some freedom to refuse particular federal conditions without jeopardizing all their federal income at one stroke. Instructional programs in science, social science, and modern languages (including English), and graduate instruction in a wide variety of fields would seem especially fit areas for federal support.

It does not seem desirable to use a massive federal scholarship program as a means of channeling federal funds into the operating budgets of educational institutions. However, a limited scholarship program (perhaps 30,000 to 50,000 scholarships a year), designed primarily to reach bright students in genuine need, does seem to be needed. Students who score high on a national ability test should be eligible for scholarships in amounts determined by their parents' taxable income and number of dependents. This scale of amounts should be such that a student from a family deemed incapable of contributing anything to his higher education receives a stipend (say $1,500) sufficient to enable him to study full time at a public institution in his state (or, if he preferred, a private institution in commuting distance). Such a program would be of no real assistance to higher educational institutions, but this would not be its purpose. Its purpose would be to reduce the number of talented students not going on to college. It should be very well advertised and highly honorific, since, hopefully, the main impact of the program would be to stimulate the high schools to encourage talented low-income students and to improve their college preparatory programs generally.

The National Defense Student Loan Fund definitely seems to be fulfilling a need, and it should be expanded and made permanent, with special emphasis on encouragement of students in professional schools to borrow when necessary to complete their courses. The forgiveness provision for school teachers seems worth continuing, so long as Congress or state legislatures do not rely on this provision as an answer to the teacher shortage. The only really satisfactory way to encourage good students to go into teaching is to make teaching an attractive career, financially and otherwise.

Similarly, graduate level federal fellowships are fulfilling a need and should be continued, but they should not be regarded as a substitute for increasing faculty salaries and making college teaching a more attractive career. The number of federal fellowships should gradually be expanded, but only as it becomes evident that there are genuinely able students who are not going to graduate school because they cannot finance it, and that there will be jobs for them at good salaries when they get out. In distributing the fellowships and support for graduate education, an effort should be made to strengthen education in places which have room for expansion and have already demonstrated a capacity for doing graduate-level work. For the next few years, it would seem much more sensible to expand and improve the existing programs of small to moderate-sized graduate departments, than to support brand new programs, especially in institutions which have not yet demonstrated a capacity for graduate level work.

SELECTED REFERENCES FOR CHAPTER 9

1) "The Federal Government and Higher Education: Findings of Regional Conferences Growing Out of the Seventeenth American Assembly," *Higher Education,* January 1961, pp. 4-7.
2) "The Federal Government and Higher Education: Resolutions and Policy Statements of Higher Education Organizations," *ibid.,* pp. 7-16.
3) The U. S. President's Science Advisory Committee, *Scientific Progress, the Universities, and the Federal Government,* November 15, 1960.

Index